HOT!

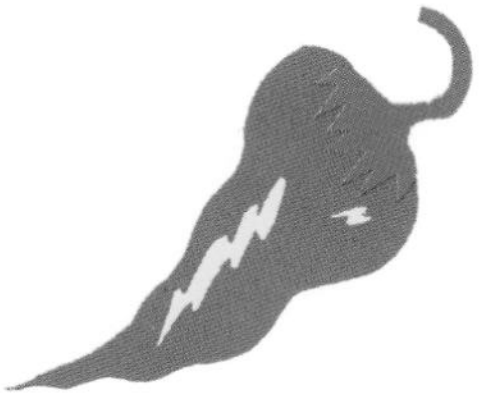

**Sautéed Cabbage and
Bow Ties** page 85

Ginger Salmon Tartar
page 23

HOT!

The Cookbook for

Passionate Devotees Who Go Bonkers

Over the Incendiary Pleasures of Food

That Never Stops Whamming, Popping, or Zapping

By Judith Choate

Photography by Amy Reichman

Illustrations by Jennifer S. Markson

Virgin

A KENAN BOOK

First published in the UK in 1992 by
Virgin Books
an imprint of Virgin Publishing
338 Ladbroke Grove
London W1O 5AH

ISBN 1 85227 379 8

HOT

The Cookbook for Passionate Devotees Who Go Bonkers Over the Incendiary Pleasures of Food That Never Stops Whamming, Popping, or Zapping
was prepared and produced by
Kenan Books, Inc.
15 West 26th Street
New York, New York 10010

Editor: Sharon Kalman
Art Director/Designer: Jeff Batzli
Photography Editor: Anne K. Price
Border Illustrations by Jennifer S. Markson
Prop Stylist: Brian Crede

Typeset by Bookworks Plus
Colour separation by United South Sea Graphic Art
Printed and bound in Hong Kong by Leefung-Asco Printers, Ltd.

Dedicated to Dean Fearing
a fellow hot fiend,
a hotter friend,
and the hottest chef

Contents

Some like it hot and some like it hotter, but I like it hottest of all! From my earliest memory of cool avocado melting into the taste of the Tex/Mex foods of my native Southwest, to more recent experiments with the sometimes blistering foods of China, India, and Southeast Asia, hot, spicy meals have remained my favourites. *Hot!* is my collection of a variety of foods from the multicoloured cuisines that offer incendiary dining pleasures.

The complexity of these zesty meals is based on the unique ability of chilles and spices to blend heat, aroma, flavour, and pungency to create a wonderfully balanced taste. Their excitement lies in the fact that their use fires both cook and diner. In fact, chilles and spices make hot foods the imaginative cook's palette upon which to create taste thrills that vibrate upon the diner's palate.

Spices are often used in combination with one another and/or with chilles to create the perfect hot proportion. For instance, the pungent sweetness of cinnamon and nutmeg is frequently used to soften the power of ginger, mustard, or chilles. The amount of heat, be it sweet or hot, in the recipes throughout this book can be modified by decreasing or increasing the aromatics. If you are new to hot foods, begin with very small doses of heat, increasing the amount as your system acclimatizes itself to your newfound fire eating. A daily diet containing searingly hot chilles can be eaten with impunity. Yet a small portion of the same chilles eaten by someone unused to them can cause blisters in the mouth

Note: All metric conversions are approximate.

and on the lips. So remember to use caution as you experience *Hot!*

Many of my recipes result from sharing the joys of cooking with food lovers from all over the world: Nino, a Peruvian lawyer-turned-kitchen steward; Faye, a Jamaican pastry chef; Dorothea, a Chinese restaurant owner; Anjan, American-born but New Delhi-fed; Ilona, Sumatra-born, Southeast Asia-travelled; and Patricia, a Bahamian home canner. These are but a few who have fed my knowledge and taste buds. Without them, my understanding of the infinite degrees of heat when cooking with spices and chilles would be without the warmth of the human dimension.

The history of the discovery and exploitation of chilles and spices is interwoven with the discovery and expansion of our world. Secrets have been sold, great wealth depleted, and thousands of lives lost in protecting the original sources of spices and chille peppers. In fact, a good many of the world's cuisines are built around the use of these aromatics. From the now-pedestrian tabletop pepper mill to the extremely expensive decorative clove, cooking with spices is the core of great dining.

Hot foods are found most frequently in hot climates. It is said that the internal heat that they create allows the body to cool in the tropical sun. Although chilles are native to the Americas, their culinary influence is felt in the far reaches of the world, so much so that it would be difficult to identify the origin of each type of chille. Equatorial countries explode with the use of spices and chilles. North Africa, Southeast Asia, the Indian continent, and Caribbean nations offer many foods that absolutely define the use of heat and spice in the creation of intriguing meals. In North America, only the American South and Southwest, with their African and Mexican heritages and warm climates, use chilles and spices as integral parts of their regional cuisine. However, some Native Americans use a liberal dose of chilles to flavour many of their traditional dishes.

Not all hot foods are searingly hot; many are quite delicate in their juxtaposition of gentle heat against cool flavour. As you expand your hot repertoire your taste buds will experience an unfolding adventure. As you go, you will learn how to create the perfect balance for your own personal hot fix. For it is true: once you brave the heat, you will become addicted to the extraordinary delights of fanning the fire.

In *Hot!* I have attempted to give you some cool, calming balance to the incendiary stars. Suggested menus with refreshing condiments and drinks combine to help create meals of a pleasing complexity, rather than those that are just powerhouses. Use your palate and imagination to expand your usual fare with the subtle shadings that spices and chilles can add. It won't take long for you to discover why some like it hot.

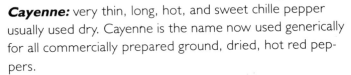

A **G**lossary of **C**hilles and **S**pices

Chilles

It is estimated that there are 2,000-plus varieties of chille peppers (genus *Capsicum*) grown throughout the world. Their heat comes from capsaicin, a chemical produced within the glands of the chille that intensifies as it matures. The heat ratio of chilles is scientifically measured in Scoville units, with peppers such as bell and sweet banana at the low end with zero Scoville units and the habañero at the high end with up to 300,000 Scoville units. When preparing chilles it is best to use rubber gloves since the seeds and oil in all hot chilles can cause intense burning. Keep your hands away from your face and eyes. If you are not using the seeds and membranes, carefully discard them out of the reach of children and animals. Rinse the cleaned pod under cool running water and pat dry. When you have finished preparing chilles, wash your gloves, hands, work surface, and utensils in warm, soapy water.

Dried chilles frequently are soaked in warm water one hour before using. Follow the above precautions when working with them as well.

The following is a list of some of the most frequently **ble** available and more commonly used chilles.

Anaheim: long green chille ranging from mild to barely hot. Dried, known as chille colorado; also called *chilles verdes*.

Ancho: long, very dark brown, mildly hot but sweet dried chille. Fresh, it is dark green and known as poblano. Best toasted before use. Also called *chille negro;* mulato.

Banana: mild yellow chille always used fresh. Bright red when very mature.

Cayenne: very thin, long, hot, and sweet chille pepper usually used dry. Cayenne is the name now used generically for all commercially prepared ground, dried, hot red peppers.

Chipotle: dried, smoked jalapeño chille. Very hot and rich, often prepared "in adobo," which is a mixture of tomatoes, onions, vinegar, and spices.

Fresno: medium-size, fairly mild, triangular-shaped chille pepper. Usually green, but mature varieties can be yellow or red.

Guajillo: long, thin, dark red, dried, very hot chille used extensively in East Indian cooking. Fresh it is known as mirasol.

Habañero: small, ridged, round, exceedingly hot and flavorful chille. Generally sold immature and green. Yellow, orange, red, and sometimes white when mature. Also called scotch bonnet.

Jalapeño: small, triangular-shaped, green, hot chille. May also be bright red when mature. Often served pickled.

Mirasol: long, thin, dark red chille used extensively in East Indian cooking. Dried known as guajillo.

New Mexico: fairly large, mildly hot, red or green chille. Used both fresh and dried.

Paprika: the bright red powder of Hungarian sweet to mildly hot chille peppers. Often used to add colour to recipes.

Pasilla: long, thin, medium, dried, hot chille.

Poblano: long, mildly hot, dark green chille. Dried known as ancho.

Serrano: small red or green very hot chille. Used fresh.

Spices

To ensure integrity of flavour, all spices should be purchased in small quantity and stored, tightly covered, in a cool, dark place. Freshly ground spices are always superior to those that are commercially ground. Purchase a small electric coffee grinder to be used solely for spice grinding. Wipe it clean after each use and allow it to air out for at least twenty-four hours to remove the odour of the most recently ground spice. You can also use a pestle and mortar to grind spices.

Allspice: ground or whole berries so named because the flavour resembles a combination of cloves, nutmeg, and cinnamon.

Anise: ground or seeds with the sweet and pungent flavour of licorice.

Caraway: seeds with a strong licorice flavour.

Cardamon: ground pods or seeds with a sweet aroma. Available green or black.

Cinnamon: ground or sticks (the rolled bark of the cinnamon tree), with a very sweet, spicy bite.

Cloves: ground or dried buds with a distinct sharp flavour.

Coriander: ground or seeds with a spicy citrus flavour. Dried coriander cannot be used in place of fresh, which is a green leafy plant also known as cilantro or Chinese parsley.

Cumin: ground or seeds with an intense, warm aroma.

Fenugreek: ground or seeds with a slightly bitter flavour.

Ginger: fresh, dried ground, or in pieces; preserved stem ginger; crystallized ginger; all have a definite hot and tangy flavour.

Mace: outer coating of nutmeg, ground or in blades with much the same warm, sweet, spicy flavour as the nut.

Mustard: ground or as yellow, brown, white, or black seeds, or in a wide variety of commercially prepared spreadable mustards with a strong, pungent taste.

Nutmeg: ground or whole fruit with a warm, sweet, spicy flavour.

Pepper: ground or whole berries, either black, white, green, or pink with a pleasant, stinging bite.

Saffron: powdered or in strands with an intense yellow colour and distinct musky flavour.

Star Anise: dried, star-shaped seed with a sweet, pungent, almost licorice taste.

Turmeric: ground with a warm, delicate flavour.

13

Blended Spice Seasonings

The following seasonings are all available commercially, with each manufacturer's blend being unique. Feel free to experiment with my basic recipes to create your own signature blends.

Hot Sauce

Makes 500mL; 16 fl oz.

Every Caribbean and Latin American cook has their favourite hot sauce. This is mine.

24 habañero chilles, stemmed and seeded

1 tomato, peeled, cored, and seeded

170g; 6 oz chopped red onion

2 cloves garlic, peeled

1 teaspoon fresh lime juice

½ teaspoon salt

325mL; 12 fl oz cider vinegar

Puree chilles, tomato, onion and garlic. Add lime juice and salt.

Heat vinegar in a small saucepan over medium heat. When hot, pour into chille mixture and process until smooth. Allow to cool. Pour into a sterilized container. Cover and store, refrigerated, for up to 6 months.

Barbecue Spice

Makes about 100g; 3½ oz.

This makes a great coating for any meat, poultry, fish, or game, grilled or baked.

10 dried ancho chilles, seeded and stemmed

2 tablespoons cumin seeds

2 teaspoons coriander seeds

½ teaspoon cloves

1 5cm; 2-inch cinnamon stick

2 tablespoons soft brown sugar

½ teaspoon dry mustard

¼ teaspoon cayenne pepper

1 tablespoon salt (or to taste)

1 teaspoon crushed black pepper

Preheat oven to Gas mark 4; 180°C; 350°F.

Place chilles, cumin and coriander seeds, cloves, and cinnamon stick on a baking sheet in preheated oven for 15 minutes or until well roasted and very aromatic. Then place in spice grinder (a small coffee grinder used only for spices) and process until smooth. You can also use a pestle and mortar to grind the spices.

Combine with remaining ingredients and store, tightly covered, in a cool place for up to 3 months.

Chille Oil

Makes 250mL; 8 fl oz.

250mL; 8 fl oz peanut or other vegetable oil

40g; ¾ oz crushed, dried, hot red chilles

Heat oil in a small saucepan over medium heat. When very hot, stir in chilles. Remove from heat and allow to cool. Pour into a sterilized container. Seal and store in a cool, dark place for up to 6 months.

Garam Masala

Makes approximately 35g; 1¼ oz.

Garam masala is an integral part of Indian cooking, yet there is no standard mixture for this aromatic seasoning. Each cook and each region has its own favourite. It can also be purchased commercially, but the flavours will be milder.

3 tablespoons cardamon seeds

1 tablespoon black peppercorns

1 5cm; 2-inch cinnamon stick

1 teaspoon whole cloves

1 teaspoon black cumin seeds (or regular cumin seeds)

½ teaspoon coriander seeds

½ teaspoon freshly ground nutmeg

1 small dried red chille, seeded

Place all ingredients in a small, clean spice grinder and process for about 30 seconds or until finely ground. Store, tightly covered, in a cool, dry place for up to 1 month.

Chinese Five-Spice Powder

Makes about 85g; 3 oz.

3 tablespoons star anise (available in Asian markets or the spice shelf in gourmet markets or some supermarkets)

2½ tablespoons fennel seeds

2 tablespoons aniseed

1 10cm; 4-inch cinnamon stick

2 tablespoons whole cloves

1 tablespoon Szechuan peppercorns (available in Asian markets or the spice shelf in gourmet markets or some supermarkets)

Process all ingredients in a spice grinder until smooth. Pour into a sterilized container with lid. Seal and store in a cool, dark place for up to 3 months.

Curry Powder

Makes approximately 600g; 1¼ pounds.

Curry powder, like garam masala, has no standard mixture. This is my basic curry powder. You can add or subtract spices depending upon your taste.

450g; 1 lb coriander seeds

120g; ¼ lb cumin seeds

1 dried hot red chille, stemmed

1 tablespoon dried ginger

1 tablespoon sweet cumin seeds (available at East Indian markets)

1 tablespoon mustard seeds

1 tablespoon fenugreek

1 5cm; 2-inch cinnamon stick

2 cardamon seeds

8 black peppercorns

1 teaspoon whole cloves

Preheat oven to Gas mark ½; 130°C; 250°F.

Place all ingredients on baking sheet with sides in preheated oven and roast for 20 minutes. Immediately put into blender or spice grinder and process at high speed until spices are very fine. Pour into a sterilized container with lid and store in cool, dark place for up to 3 months.

Chapter One

Hors d'**O**euvres and **A**ppetizers

Vegetable **S**amosas with **C**oriander **D**ipping **S**auce

Tom's **H**ot **C**hille **P**eppers with **A**nchovies

Coconut **P**rawns with **C**alypso **P**unch

Ginger **S**almon **T**artare

Chille **S**eviche with **T**ostones

Cocktail **C**hicken **K**ebabs

Laab

Jalapeño **C**heddar **R**ajas

Savannah **C**heese **W**afers

Middle **E**astern **S**picy **W**alnut **S**pread

Vegetable Samosas with Coriander Dipping Sauce

Makes about 1½ dozen.

Samosas, a much-loved traditional East Indian snack, may be made with any meat, poultry, or vegetable filling you desire.

1 teaspoon Garam Masala (see page 13)

1 teaspoon ground cumin

1 teaspoon ground coriander

½ teaspoon ground turmeric

120mL; 8 fl oz vegetable oil

85g; 3 oz chopped red onion

1 clove garlic, peeled and chopped

1 fresh hot green chille, stemmed and chopped

2 teaspoons minced fresh ginger

3 tablespoons fresh orange juice

170g; 6 oz chopped cooked potatoes

70g; 2½ oz frozen petit pois, thawed and patted dry

225g; 8 oz chopped cooked spinach

85g; 3 oz chopped cooked turnips (or parsnips)

½ teaspoon cayenne pepper (or to taste)

Salt (to taste)

285g; 10 oz sifted plain flour

60mL; 2 fl oz warm water

Approximately 500mL; 16 fl oz peanut oil

Coriander Dipping Sauce

Place Garam Masala, cumin, coriander, and turmeric in a small nonstick frying pan over medium heat. Fry, stirring constantly, for about 3 minutes or until spices just begin to brown. Immediately remove from heat and set aside.

Heat 50mL of the vegetable oil in a medium-size sauté pan over medium-high heat. When hot, add red onion and garlic. Fry, stirring constantly, for about 5 minutes or until the mixture just begins to brown. Stir in chille, ginger, and orange juice. Cover and cook for 3 minutes. Remove cover and stir in potatoes, peas, spinach, and turnips. When well combined, add roasted spices and season with cayenne pepper and salt. Lower heat, cover, and cook for 5 minutes. Add 1 tablespoon of water at a time if mixture seems too dry. Remove from heat and allow to stand until cool.

Combine flour, salt to taste, and 60mL; 2 fl oz vegetable oil in a food processor fitted with the metal blade. Process until coarse crumbs are formed. Add warm water, a bit at a time, to make a stiff, smooth dough. Combine dough into a ball, rub with remaining oil, and cover

tightly. Allow to set for 30 minutes.

Divide the dough into 9 balls. On a lightly floured surface, roll out 1 ball at a time into circles about 15cm; 6 inches in diameter, keeping other balls well covered to prevent them from drying out. Cut each circle in half, then fold the edges in toward each other to form a cone shape (similar to a coffee filter), allowing edges to overlap slightly. Place a bit of water along cut edge and press to seal. Place about 2 tablespoons of the vegetable mixture into pocket, then seal the rounded edges together with a bit of water to make dough sticky, if necessary. Use thumb and forefinger to flute the edges.

Heat peanut oil in a deep-fry pan over medium heat. When just hot, add samosas a few at a time and fry, turning frequently, until golden on both sides. Drain on paper towels. Serve hot or at room temperature with Coriander Dipping Sauce or Cucumber Yogurt with Mint and Coriander (page 115).

Coriander Dipping Sauce

Makes approximately 250mL; 8 fl oz.

85g; 3 oz fresh cilantro leaves

2 tablespoons fresh mint leaves

1 small hot green chille of choice, stemmed (or to taste)

2 tablespoons fresh orange juice

½ teaspoon fresh lime juice

Salt (to taste)

Combine all ingredients in a blender or a food processor fitted with the metal blade. Process until smooth. Pour into a nonreactive container. Cover and refrigerate until ready to serve.

Tom's Hot Chille Peppers with Anchovies

I don't believe that I've ever seen a printed recipe for this very hot appetizer, which is often used as a part of an antipasto. This comes from Suzy, a third-generation Italian-American, whose grandfather taught her to make it. To make this recipe, you will need a clay crock with a wooden block that fits down into the crock.

½ bushel hot anaheim or other long, green, hot chilles (approximately 125 chilles)

2 anchovy fillets per chille (approximately 250 fillets)

Approximately 700g; 1½ lb salt

Olive oil

Wash chilles. Using gloves, remove stems. Split lengthwise down one side. Place 2 anchovies inside each split chille. Carefully place chilles in the crock in neat layers with about 170g; 6 oz salt over each layer.

When crock is full, place wooden block on chilles and top with a heavy stone to create pressure that will eliminate liquid. The salt will extract water, which will preserve the chilles. It will take at least 2 full days to extract all of the liquid. Be certain to empty the crock each day. When no liquid can be poured off, cover chilles with olive oil to come up 1cm; ½ inch above them. Cover crock again with the wood block. Store in a cool, dry place for at least 3 months before eating. After 3 months, chilles can be removed from the crock and placed in sterilized jars covered with olive oil from the crock. Seal and store up to 6 months in a cool, dark place or in the refrigerator.

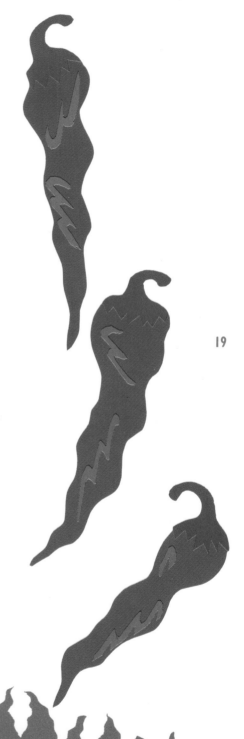

19

Coconut Prawns with Calypso Punch

Serves 6.

This is a family favourite, combining many of our favourite hot and sweet flavours.

1 kg; 2 lb large prawns with tails on, peeled and deveined

4 eggs (size 3)

120mL; 4 fl oz honey

2 teaspoons cayenne pepper

½ teaspoon Hot Sauce (see page 12)

220g; 7½ oz sifted plain flour

70g; 2½ oz cornflour

1 tablespoon Curry Powder

285g; 10 oz fine bread crumbs

200g; 7 oz unsweetened grated coconut

1 tablespoon grated orange zest

Approximately 1.2L; 2 pt rapeseed oil

Calypso Punch

Wash and dry prawns. Set aside.

Beat eggs, honey, cayenne pepper, and Hot Sauce together. When well beaten, pour into a shallow bowl. Combine flour, cornflour, and Curry Powder in a shallow bowl. Then, combine bread crumbs, coconut, and orange zest in a third bowl. Dip each prawn into egg mixture, then the flour mixture. Again dip into the egg mixture and finally in the coconut bread crumbs. Set aside.

Heat oil to 165°C; 325°F in a deep-fry pan over medium-high heat. When temperature is reached, add coconut prawns a few at a time and fry for about 3 minutes or until golden. Drain on paper towels. Serve hot with Calypso Punch on the side.

Calypso Punch

Makes approximately 700mL; 24 fl oz.

160g; 5½ oz finely diced fresh pineapple

1 orange, segments finely diced

115g; 4 oz finely diced jicama

30g; 1 oz finely diced red onion

1 tablespoon fresh lime juice

1 tablespoon minced fresh ginger

1 tablespoon minced fresh mint

1 tablespoon finely chopped jalapeño chille (optional)

1 tablespoon honey

Salt (to taste)

Combine all ingredients in a nonreactive bowl. Cover and allow to marinate 30 minutes before serving.

Ginger Salmon Tartare

Serves 6.

A taste of the Orient in a very pretty appetizer that I often use for a formal dinner.

450g; I lb smoked salmon

170g; 6 oz raw, skinless, boneless salmon fillets

2 hard-boiled eggs, finely chopped

2 tablespoons grated onion

½ teaspoon minced serrano chille

3 tablespoons minced pickled ginger (available in Asian markets)

I teaspoon grated fresh ginger

I teaspoon fresh lemon juice

Salt (to taste)

4 pickling cucumbers

I large daikon (or white Chinese radish) (available in Asian markets)

I medium red onion

3 tablespoons rice wine vinegar (available in Asian markets)

2 tablespoons caster sugar

¼ teaspoon cayenne pepper

¼ teaspoon crushed Szechuan peppercorns (available in Asian markets)

½ large cucumber

115g; 4 oz softened butter

24 4cm; I½-inch toast rounds

2 tablespoons black caviar

Chill 6 large salad plates.

Coarsely chop salmon together. Place in medium-size nonreactive bowl. Stir in eggs, grated onion, chille, I½ tablespoons pickled ginger, fresh ginger, and lemon juice. Stir until well combined but not mushy. Cover and refrigerate for at least 30 minutes. When well chilled, taste and add salt if necessary.

Wash and dry pickling cucumbers. Cut into a fine julienne and generously sprinkle with salt. Place in a fine sieve and allow to drain for 20 minutes. Rinse under cold running water and pat dry. Set aside.

Peel daikon and cut into a fine julienne. Peel and cut red onion into a fine julienne. Place drained cucumbers and vegetables in a nonreactive bowl. Toss with remaining pickled ginger, rice wine vinegar, sugar, cayenne pepper, salt to taste, and peppercorns. Allow the relish to marinate at least 30 minutes.

Cut cucumber into very fine slices. Generously butter toast rounds and cover with a thin layer of cucumber slices.

Pack chilled salmon mixture into 6 small moulds, no larger than 120mL; 4 fl oz. Unmould I salmon round into the centre of each of the 6 chilled plates. Surround one side of the salmon round with 4 cucumber toasts and the other side with cucumber relish. Sprinkle top of salmon with black caviar and serve immediately.

22

Chille Seviche with Tostones

Serves 6.

Many versions of seviche are found throughout Latin America. I combine my version with tostones, the potato crisp of these regions.

900g; 2 lb scallops, or firm, skinless, boneless fish fillets, or shelled oysters, or any combination thereof

250mL; 8 fl oz fresh lemon juice

180mL; 6 fl oz fresh lime juice

120mL; 4 fl oz bitter (or Seville) orange juice (available in Latin-American or Caribbean markets)

230g; 8 oz diced, peeled fresh tomatoes

2 to 3 fresh, hot, red or green chille peppers (or to taste), sliced thin

170g; 6 oz diced red onion

40g; 1½ oz chopped spring onion, including green part

1 teaspoon minced garlic

½ teaspoon cracked black pepper

Salt (to taste)

Tostones

230g; 8 oz diced red pepper

Cut scallops (if necessary) or fish into bite-size pieces. Place in a nonreactive bowl and add lemon and lime juice to cover (use additional juice if necessary). Cover and refrigerate for at least 6 hours, turning at least 2 times. The citrus juice will "cook" the fish. Drain well.

Combine marinated fish with orange juice, tomatoes, chilles, onion, spring onion, garlic, pepper, and salt. Allow to marinate for 30 minutes.

Place equal portions of Seviche on each of 6 plates, placing 3 Tostones per plate to one side, and garnish with red pepper. Serve immediately.

Tostones

Makes approximately 18 tostones.

1 large green plantain (or green banana) (available in Latin-American or Caribbean markets)

Approximately 1.2L; 2 pt vegetable oil

Salt (to taste)

Peel plantain and slice on the bias into 1cm; ½-inch slices. Place in cold, salted water to cover for 30 minutes. Drain and pat dry.

Make a fresh bowl of cold, salted water.

Heat oil in a deep-fry pan over medium heat to 165°C; 325°F on a food thermometer. Fry the plantains, a few at a time, for about 5 minutes or until tender. Place on paper towels to drain. Cover with brown or grease proof paper and press to flatten slightly. When all slices are tenderized and flattened, raise oil to 190°C; 375°F on a food thermometer. Dip the flattened plantains into cold, salted water and flick off excess liquid. Immediately drop into hot oil, being careful of splattering. Fry for about 1 minute or until crisp. Drain on paper towels and sprinkle with salt. Serve immediately.

Cocktail Chicken Kebabs

Serves 6.

Indian seasonings enliven these tasty cocktail tidbits.

These can be adapted easily to main course kebabs by cutting the chicken into larger pieces and adding chunks of pepper and baby onions to a large skewer. Be sure to brush the vegetables with some of the marinade.

3 whole boneless, skinless chicken breasts

3 tablespoons fresh lemon juice

115g; 4 oz plain yoghurt

1 tablespoon minced garlic

1 tablespoon minced fresh ginger

1 dried hot red chille, stemmed

1 teaspoon ground cumin

¼ teaspoon ground turmeric

¼ teaspoon Garam Masala (see page 13)

Pinch saffron

Salt (to taste)

115g; 4 oz clarified butter (see note below)

Cut the chicken into bite-size pieces. Place in a nonreactive bowl and toss with lemon juice. Cover and set aside for 30 minutes.

Combine yoghurt, garlic, ginger, chille, cumin, turmeric, Garam Masala, saffron, and salt in a food processor fitted with the metal blade. When smooth, pour over chicken pieces. Toss to combine. Cover and refrigerate for at least 3 hours, but no more than 24 hours.

Soak rounded wooden cocktail sticks in cold water for 1 hour. Drain well.

Preheat oven to 260°C; 500°F.

Place 1 piece of chicken on each soaked cocktail stick. Brush chicken with clarified butter and place on a baking sheet with sides. When all chicken pieces are skewered, place in preheated oven for about 4 minutes or until just cooked. Serve immediately.

Note: To clarify butter, melt cold butter over low heat. When melted, allow to set about 5 minutes, then pour clear yellow liquid off and discard the solids. The butter can be used immediately or covered tightly and stored, refrigerated, for 1 week, or frozen for 6 months.

Laab

Serves 6.

You may substitute any minced meat or poultry for the beef in this traditional Thai snack. However, you may need to add some vegetable oil when browning if you're using a very lean meat or poultry.

450g; 1 lb lean minced beef

2 tablespoons minced garlic

2 tablespoons minced shallots

3 tablespoons minced red onion

2 tablespoons minced spring onion, including green part

2 tablespoons chopped fresh coriander

3 tablespoons chopped fresh mint

2 tablespoons minced, fresh, hot red chilles

3 tablespoons fresh lime juice

2 tablespoons Thai fish sauce (available in Asian markets)

Salt (to taste)

24 small Butterhead lettuce leaves, washed and dried

24 whole mint leaves

Place minced beef, garlic, and shallots in a nonstick frying pan over medium-high heat. Fry, stirring frequently, for about 8 minutes or until quite brown. Remove from heat and scrape into a bowl. Let sit for 15 minutes, then stir in red onion, spring onion, coriander, mint, chilles, lime juice, and fish sauce to combine. Taste and adjust seasonings with salt if necessary.

Spoon equal portions of the meat mixture into each lettuce leaf. Top with a mint leaf and fold lettuce leaf around filling. Serve immediately.

Jalapeño Cheddar Rajas

Serves 6.

This is like a Mexican version of fondue.

6 poblano chilles

1 large onion

2 tablespoons rapeseed oil

1 clove garlic, peeled and minced

250mL; 8 fl oz double cream

60g; 2 oz grated mild cheddar cheese

1 tablespoon minced jalepeño chille

2 tablespoons chopped fresh coriander

8 warm corn or flour tortillas, quartered

Preheat grill.

Lay chilles on a baking sheet or grill pan. Place under preheated grill and cook, turning frequently, until skin is charred. Remove from heat and place in a plastic bag. Seal and let stand for 15 minutes.

Using gloves, remove chilles and push skin off. Cut into quarters lengthwise, stem, and remove seeds.

Peel onion and cut in half lengthwise, then into julienne strips.

Heat oil in a heavy frying pan over medium-high heat. When hot, add onion and garlic. Lower heat and sauté for about 5 minutes or until onion is very soft but not brown. Add chilles and cream. Simmer for about 12 minutes or until thickened. Remove from heat and stir in cheese and coriander. Serve immediately using warm tortillas as scoops.

Savannah Cheese Wafers

Makes about 3 dozen.

115g; 4 oz butter

115g; 4 oz grated sharp cheddar cheese

285g; 10 oz plain flour

½ teaspoon baking powder

½ teaspoon salt

1½ teaspoons cayenne pepper (or to taste)

Dash Hot Sauce (see page 12) (optional)

140g; 5 oz sesame seeds

Cream butter and cheese until smooth. Add flour, baking powder, salt, cayenne pepper, and Hot Sauce and blend into a smooth dough. Do not over-beat.

Divide dough in half and shape into 2 logs about 3cm; 1¼ inch in diameter. Roll each log in sesame seeds to thoroughly coat. Wrap in cling film and refrigerate for at least 2 hours. (Dough also may be frozen and thawed before baking.)

Preheat oven to Gas mark 6; 205°C; 400°F.

Cut chilled logs into 0.3cm; ⅛-inch slices and lay on an ungreased baking sheet, about 2.5cm; 1 inch apart. Place in preheated oven and bake for about 10 minutes or until golden. Serve warm or at room temperature.

Middle **E**astern **S**picy **W**alnut **S**pread

Makes approximately 470mL, 16 fl oz.

225g; 8 oz chopped walnuts

140g; 5 oz extra-fine bread crumbs

½ teaspoon minced fresh hot green chille

2 tablespoons fresh lemon juice

2 tablespoons fresh orange juice

1 teaspoon paprika

1 teaspoon ground cumin

¼ teaspoon cayenne pepper

2 tablespoons peanut oil

1 tablespoon cracked black pepper

2 tablespoons minced fresh parsley

Combine walnuts, bread crumbs, chille, lemon and orange juices, paprika, cumin, cayenne pepper, and peanut oil in a food processor fitted with the metal blade, using quick on-and-off turns. Add no more than 60mL; 2 fl oz water, a bit at a time, if necessary, to reach spreading consistency.

Scrape into a serving bowl and sprinkle with cracked pepper and parsley. Serve as a cocktail spread with toasted pita quarters or other Middle Eastern toasts or crackers, if desired.

Chapter Two

Soups and Salads

Spicy Lime Chicken Soup

Callalou with Foo-Foo

Curried Pumpkin Soup

Corn Chowder with Jalapeño Corn Muffins

Ginger Consommé

Barbecued Chicken Salad

Stir-Fried Beef on Bitter Greens with Chille Vinaigrette

Gado Gado

Yellow Beetroot, Mangetout, and Jicama Salad

Szechuan Slaw

Spicy Lime Chicken Soup

Serves 6 to 8.

This soup combines the flavours of two of my favorite cuisines: Mexican and Thai.

1.2L; 2 pt chicken stock

60g; 2 oz chopped shallots

1 tomato, cored and chopped

½ yellow pepper, seeded and chopped

2 stalks lemongrass (available in Asian markets)

1 tablespoon minced fresh ginger

1 fresh serrano chille, stemmed and seeded

6 kaffir lime leaves, shredded (available in Asian markets)

2 whole boneless, skinless chicken breasts, halved

1 tablespoon fresh lime juice

Salt (to taste)

Pepper (to taste)

2 tablespoons chopped fresh coriander

Fried Tortilla Crisps

Seasoned Chille Sauce

Combine the chicken stock, shallots, tomato, pepper, lemongrass, ginger, chille, and kaffir lime leaves in a heavy saucepan over high heat. Bring to a boil. Lower heat and simmer for 20 minutes. Add chicken breasts and continue to cook for 15 minutes or until chicken is cooked through. Remove chicken breasts. Shred meat and set aside.

Strain broth through a fine sieve. Season with lime juice, salt, and pepper. Return to heat if necessary to warm to serving temperature.

Place an equal portion of shredded chicken in each of 6 soup bowls. Pour in broth. Garnish with coriander and Fried Tortilla Crisps, and pass Seasoned Chille Sauce, if desired.

Fried Tortilla Crisps

Makes approximately 470mL; 2 cups.

6 corn tortillas

250mL; 8 fl oz vegetable oil

Cut tortillas into 3mm; ⅛-inch strips. Heat oil in a heavy frying pan over medium-high heat. When hot, add tortilla strips a few at a time and fry until crisp. Drain well on paper towels.

Seasoned Chille Sauce

Makes approximately 240mL; 8 fl oz.

120mL; 4 fl oz fresh lime juice

4 fresh hot red chilles

3 cloves garlic, peeled

2 tablespoons minced fresh coriander

2 teaspoons caster sugar

60mL; 2 fl oz Thai fish sauce (available in Asian markets)

Combine all ingredients in a blender to make a smooth paste. The sauce may be stored in a nonreactive container, covered and refrigerated, for up to 3 days.

Callalou with Foo-Foo

Serves 6 to 8.

I was first introduced to callalou by a Trinidadian friend who had travelled throughout the Caribbean and added ingredients from every island to his version of this very tasty Creole soup. The essential ingredient is callalou, the leaf of a variety of tropical, edible tuber. Since it is difficult to find callalou outside its normal habitat, fresh Chinese spinach or chard will give you almost the same flavour. For complete authenticity serve this soup with Foo-Foo, its traditional accompaniment.

2 small ham knuckles or trotters

900g; 2 lb fresh callalou leaves (or fresh Chinese spinach or chard)

115g; ¼ lb salt pork

170g; 6 oz chopped onion

2 teaspoons minced garlic

450g; 1 lb cubed potatoes

60g; 2 oz chopped spring onion, including green part

1 whole habañero chille (or chille of choice)

1 teaspoon minced fresh thyme

1 bay leaf

2L; 64 fl oz chicken stock

225g; ½ lb fresh okra, sliced

120mL; 4 fl oz Coconut Milk (see page 119)

350g; 12 oz mixed fresh fish and shellfish, such as crab, lobsters, and scallops

Juice of 1 lime

Salt (to taste)

Pepper (to taste)

Hot Sauce (to taste) (see page 12)

Scrub ham hocks. Place in cold water to cover and let stand for at least 4 hours. Drain. Place in a deep saucepan with water to cover. Bring to a boil over high heat. Boil for 5 minutes, then remove from heat and drain well.

Wash and dry greens thoroughly. Coarsely chop and set aside.

Cut the salt pork into bite-size pieces. Place in a small frying pan over medium heat. Fry, stirring frequently, for about 10 minutes or until most of the fat has been rendered out. Pour off all but 1 tablespoon of the fat. Add onion and garlic and continue to fry, stirring frequently, for about 4 minutes or until very soft. Scrape into saucepan with the ham knuckles. Add greens, potatoes, spring onion, chille, herbs, and chicken stock to the pot. Return to medium heat and bring to a boil. When boiling, lower heat to a simmer and cook for 45 minutes. Stir in okra, Coconut Milk, and shellfish. Cook for an additional 15 minutes. Add lime juice. Taste and adjust seasonings with salt, pepper, and Hot Sauce, if desired. Serve immediately with Foo-Foo on the side or in the soup.

Foo-Foo

Makes approximately 18.

3 green plantains (available in Latin-American or Caribbean markets)

30g; 1 oz butter

Salt (to taste)

Place the plantains, skin on, in cold water to cover in a medium-size saucepan over high heat. Bring to a boil. Boil for about 40 minutes or until tender. Drain.

Peel plantains and cut into small pieces. Puree in a food processor fitted with the metal blade until quite smooth, adding hot water a spoonful at a time if mixture gets too dry and sticky. Beat in butter and salt. Form into small 2.5cm; 1-inch balls and keep warm until ready to serve.

Curried Pumpkin Soup

Serves 6 to 8.

This soup may be served hot or cold, and can be made with any winter squash in place of the pumpkin.

30g; I oz butter

170g; 6 oz chopped onion

60g; 2 oz chopped shallots

I clove garlic, peeled and chopped

I kg; 2½ lb cubed fresh pumpkin (about a 2 kg; 4 lb pumpkin)

I tart apple, peeled, cored, and chopped

IL; 32 fl oz chicken broth

250mL; 8 fl oz fresh orange juice

2 tablespoons Curry Powder (see page 13)

I teaspoon minced fresh dill

I teaspoon grated orange zest

250mL; 8 fl oz double cream

Coriander Chutney

Melt butter in a large saucepan over medium heat. When melted, add onion, shallots, and garlic. Cook, stirring frequently, for 5 minutes or until vegetables are soft. Add pumpkin, apple, chicken broth, orange juice, Curry Powder, dill, and orange zest. Bring to a boil. Lower heat and simmer for about 40 minutes or until pumpkin is very soft. Drain, reserving liquid.

Puree in batches in a blender or a food processor fitted with the metal blade, adding reserved liquid as necessary to make a thick puree. When pureed, stir in double cream. If necessary, return to heat to just warm through. Do not boil. Pour into warm soup bowls and garnish with Coriander Chutney.

Coriander Chutney

Makes about 240mL; 8 fl oz.

40g; I½ oz fresh coriander leaves

½ yellow pepper, stemmed, seeded, and chopped

I fresh hot red chille, stemmed, seeded, and chopped

40g; I½ oz roasted, unsalted pumpkin seeds

½ teaspoon roasted cumin seeds

I teaspoon fresh orange juice ·

Combine all ingredients in a blender or a food processor fitted with the metal blade, pushing down to combine. Add additional roasted pumpkin seeds if the chutney is too thin. Store, covered and refrigerated, for up to I day, until ready to use.

Corn Chowder with Jalapeño Corn Muffins

Serves 6 to 8.

This chowder is as colourful as it is flavourful. The secret is to dice all of the vegetables to the same size as the sweetcorn.

40g; I½ oz butter

40g; I½ oz chopped onion

30g; I oz chopped celery

I clove garlic

500g; 18 oz fresh sweetcorn (or frozen, thawed, and well drained)

IL; 32 fl oz chicken stock

170g; 6 oz finely diced sweet potatoes

70g; 2½ oz finely diced red pepper

70g; 2½ oz finely diced green pepper

60g; 2 oz finely diced fennel

I tablespoon fresh lime juice

Salt (to taste)

Cayenne pepper (to taste)

250mL; 8 fl oz double cream

Jalapeño Corn Muffins

Melt butter in a heavy saucepan over medium-high heat. When melted, add onion, celery, and garlic. Cook, stirring frequently, for 5 minutes. Add 340g; 12 oz of the sweetcorn and chicken stock. Bring to a boil. When boiling, lower heat and simmer for 30 minutes. Remove from heat and puree in batches in a blender or a food processor fitted with the metal blade. Strain puree through a fine sieve into a clean saucepan. Stir in remaining sweetcorn, sweet potatoes, peppers, and fennel and bring to a boil over high heat. When boiling, lower heat and simmer for 10 minutes or until vegetables are cooked but still firm. Season to taste with lime juice, salt, and pepper.

Stir in double cream a bit at a time until serving consistency is reached. Serve immediately with warm Jalapeño Corn Muffins.

Jalapeño Corn Muffins

Makes approximately 36 miniature muffins.

115g; 4 oz yellow cornmeal (polenta)

140g; 5 oz plain flour

1 tablespoon baking powder

2 teaspoons caster sugar

¼ teaspoon salt

1 jalapeño chille, stemmed, seeded, and minced

1 egg (size 3)

30g; 1 oz melted butter

355mL; 12 fl oz buttermilk

Preheat oven to Gas mark 7; 220°C; 425°F.

Generously grease miniature muffin tins. Combine dry ingredients. Stir in chille. Whisk together egg, melted butter, and buttermilk and stir into dry ingredients. Do not overmix.

Fill prepared tins about three-quarters full. Place in preheated oven and bake for about 10 minutes or until light brown. Serve warm.

Ginger Consommé

Serves 6 to 8.

Asian flavours add zip to an ordinary clear soup.

This soup can be served either hot or cold.

2L; 64 fl oz unsalted defatted chicken stock

115g; 4 oz chopped fresh ginger

30g; 1 oz chopped shallots

2 tablespoons fresh lemon juice

1 stalk lemongrass (available in Asian markets)

1 carrot, peeled and chopped

1 sliced fresh hot green chille

2 tablespoons minced fresh parsley

Salt (to taste)

White pepper (to taste)

1 tablespoon minced fresh coriander

Place chicken stock, ginger, shallots, lemon juice, lemongrass, carrot, chille, and 1 tablespoon parsley in a heavy saucepan over high heat. Bring to a boil. When boiling, lower heat and simmer for 45 minutes. Remove from heat and let stand for at least 1 hour.

Strain through a double layer of muslin and discard solids. Taste and adjust seasonings with salt and white pepper. Serve at room temperature, cold or hot, garnished with remaining parsley and coriander.

Barbecued Chicken Salad

Serves 6.

A little bit of the South and a little bit of the Southwest combine to make this special chicken salad.

2 ancho chilles

3 shallots, peeled

120mL; 4 fl oz orange blossom honey

60mL; 2 fl oz raspberry vinegar

80mL; 2½ fl oz rapeseed oil

½ teaspoon dry mustard

2 tablespoons Barbecue Spice (see page 12)

Salt (to taste)

Pepper (to taste)

500g; 18 oz cooked and drained black-eyed peas

115g; 4 oz diced green pepper

45g; 1½ oz diced red onion

60g; 2 oz cornmeal (cornmeal may be replaced by polenta or grits cooked according to package directions, then set, sliced and grilled as for cornmeal)

10g; ¼ oz butter

30g; 1 oz melted butter

3 whole boneless, skinless chicken breasts, split

1 tablespoon olive oil

Juice of 1 lemon

Fried Tortilla Crisps (see page 27)

Place chilles in boiling water to cover for 10 minutes or until soft. Drain and remove stems.

Process chilles, shallots, honey, vinegar, oil, dry mustard, and 1 teaspoon Barbecue Spice in a blender until smooth. Add salt and pepper.

Combine black-eyed peas, pepper, and red onion in a nonreactive bowl. Pour dressing over all and stir to combine. Set aside to marinate at room temperature for at least 1 hour.

Pour cornmeal into 500mL; 16 fl oz rapidly boiling water. Stir in salt and 10g; ¼ oz butter. Return to a boil. When boiling, lower heat and simmer, stirring constantly, for about 15 minutes or until quite thick. Pour into a buttered 15cm; 6-inch loaf tin and allow to set until firm. When firm, cut into 1cm; ½-inch-thick slices. Brush with melted butter and sprinkle with approximately 1 teaspoon Barbecue Spice. Set aside.

Rub chicken breasts with olive oil and lemon juice.

Preheat barbecue or grill.

Generously coat all sides of the chicken with remaining Barbecue Spice. Place on pre-heated barbecue (or under grill) and cook for about 5 minutes per side or until chicken is just cooked through. Four minutes before the chicken is ready, put the seasoned cornmeal slices on the barbecue or under the grill, cooking 2 minutes per side.

Slice each chicken breast on the bias and fan out on each of 6 warm salad plates. Cut cornmeal slices in half on the diagonal and place one triangle at the twelve, three, six, and nine o'clock positions on the plate. Place a spoonful of black-eyed peas between each triangle. Drizzle black-eyed pea dressing over top of chicken and sprinkle entire salad with Fried Tortilla Crisps. Serve immediately.

Stir-Fried Beef on Bitter Greens with Chille Vinaigrette

Serves 6.

This Asian-flavoured salad also makes a zesty brunch or luncheon main course.

450g; 1 lb very lean fillet of beef

3 dried Chinese mushrooms

1 chipotle chille

120mL; 4 fl oz hoisin sauce (available in Asian markets)

60mL; 2 fl oz tamari soy sauce (available in Asian markets)

1 teaspoon minced garlic

1 tablespoon rice wine vinegar (available in Asian markets)

1 teaspoon light soft brown sugar

1 5cm; 2-inch cinnamon stick

2 tablespoons rapeseed oil

4mL; 12 cups mixed bitter greens (watercress, radicchio, curly endive, and chicory)

85g; 3 oz julienned sweet onions (such as Vidalia or Maui)

Chille Vinaigrette

30g; 1 oz chopped fresh chiyes

Slice beef into thin strips about 5cm; 2 inches long and 2.5cm; 1 inch wide. Set aside.

Soak mushrooms and chille in boiling water to cover for 15 minutes. Drain, discarding liquid. Trim tough stems from mushrooms, cut into a fine julienne, and set aside. Process chille, hoisin sauce, soy sauce, garlic, rice wine vinegar, and sugar in a blender until smooth. Place beef and mushrooms in a nonreactive bowl and pour chille mixture on top. Cover and refrigerate for 1 hour.

Heat 1 tablespoon oil in a wok over high heat. When hot, add beef mixture with any marinade. Stir-fry for about 2 minutes or until beef is just beginning to brown. Remove from wok and add remaining oil. When hot, quickly add greens to wok and stir-fry for about 1 minute or until just wilting and coated with oil.

Immediately place equal portions of greens on each of 6 warm salad plates (or 1 large serving platter). Top with equal portions of beef and mushrooms. Drizzle with Chille Vinaigrette and sprinkle with chives. Serve immediately.

Chille Vinaigrette

Makes about 120mL; 4 fl oz.

60mL; 2 fl oz rice wine vinegar (available in Asian markets)

3 tablespoons fresh lime juice

1 tablespoon fresh orange juice

3 tablespoons pure maple syrup

1 tablespoon chille paste (available in Asian markets)

1 tablespoon minced shallots

1 tablespoon minced fresh hot red chilles

1 tablespoon minced fresh coriander

½ teaspoon grated orange zest

Salt (to taste)

Pepper (to taste)

Whisk all ingredients together until well combined. Add orange juice or water, 1 tablespoon at a time, if dressing seems too thick.

Gado Gado

Serves 6 to 8.

This is the star of Indonesian cooking. It is always bountiful—a beautiful bowl filled to the brim with fresh and tasty foods. You may use any vegetable you wish in putting together Gado Gado.

700g; 1½ lb tofu (firm soybean cakes)

1 tablespoon vegetable oil

140g; 5 oz shredded carrot

115g; 4 oz French-cut green beans

115g; 4 oz shredded green cabbage

115g; 4 oz shredded red cabbage

60g; 2 oz shredded spinach

140g; 5 oz julienned cooked potatoes

115g; 4 oz julienned cucumber

85g; 3 oz bean sprouts

3 hard-boiled eggs, peeled and sliced crosswise

2 ripe tomatoes, cored and sliced crosswise

Warm Peanut Sauce

Crispy Onions

Cut tofu into 1cm; ½-inch cubes. Pat dry.

Heat oil in a medium-size frying pan over medium heat. When hot, add tofu and fry, stirring constantly, for about 4 minutes or until tofu has browned on all sides. Remove from pan and drain on paper towels. Set aside.

Blanch the carrots and green beans in rapidly boiling salted water. Immediately shock in cold water. Drain well and pat dry. Set aside.

Combine the cabbages and spinach and place on the bottom of a large, round, see-through serving dish. Make a layer of green beans, then potatoes, then cucumbers, then carrots, and finally bean sprouts. Alternate slices of egg and tomato around the outside edge. Sprinkle with tofu. Pour Warm Peanut Sauce over top and garnish with Crispy Onions.

Warm Peanut Sauce

Makes approximately 470mL; 16 fl oz.

250mL; 8 fl oz Coconut Milk (see page 114)

180mL; 6 fl oz smooth peanut butter

1 teaspoon minced garlic

1 fresh hot red chille, stemmed and chopped

1 teaspoon shrimp paste (available in Asian markets)

1 tablespoon light soft brown sugar

1 tablespoon soy sauce

2 tablespoons fresh lemon juice

1 5cm; 2-inch piece lemon peel

1 teaspoon tamarind (available in Asian markets), dissolved in 1 tablespoon warm water

Combine Coconut Milk, peanut butter, garlic, chille, shrimp paste, brown sugar, soy sauce, lemon juice, lemon peel, and tamarind in a medium-size saucepan over medium-high heat. Bring to a boil. Lower heat and simmer for 5 minutes. Add warm water, 1 tablespoon at a time, if sauce seems too thick. Remove lemon peel and pour sauce into a blender or a food processor fitted with the metal blade. Process until smooth. Set aside and keep warm until ready to use.

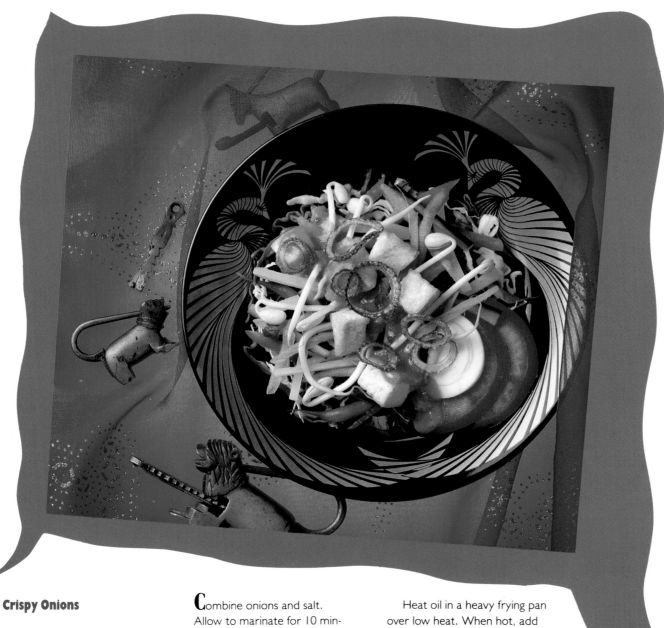

Crispy Onions

Makes about 250mL; 8 fl oz.

230g; 8 oz thinly sliced small baby onions

1 teaspoon salt

250mL; 8 fl oz rapeseed oil

Combine onions and salt. Allow to marinate for 10 minutes. Place between layers of paper towels and squeeze out all liquid.

Heat oil in a heavy frying pan over low heat. When hot, add onions and cook, stirring constantly, for about 10 minutes or until onions are light brown. Do not overcook. Place on paper towels to drain until crisp, about 20 minutes. The onions may be stored, tightly covered, for up to 2 days.

Yellow Beetroot, Mangetout, and Jicama Salad

Serves 6.

My special salad—colourful, delicious, and flavourful.

700g; 1½ lb fresh yellow beetroots

I tablespoon olive oil

230g; ½ lb fresh mangetout

230g; ½ lb jicama (celery root or fennel may be substituted)

180mL; 6 fl oz fresh orange juice

2 tablespoons fresh lemon juice

60mL; 2 fl oz rice wine vinegar (available in Asian markets)

180mL; 6 fl oz peanut oil

I tablespoon sesame oil (available in Asian markets)

I teaspoon grated orange rind

¼ teaspoon cayenne pepper

Salt (to taste)

White pepper (to taste)

I head Butterhead lettuce, trimmed, washed, and dried

30g; I oz chive blossoms or other edible flowers

Preheat oven to Gas mark 4; 180°C; 350°F.

Trim beetroots and rub with olive oil. Place on a rack in a roasting pan filled with about Icm; ½ inch of water. Place in preheated oven and bake for about 30 minutes or until just cooked. Remove from oven and allow to cool. When cool, peel and cut into a fine julienne. Set aside at room temperature.

Trim mangetout. Blanch in rapidly boiling salted water for 30 seconds until crisp, tender, and bright green. Immediately pour into a strainer and shock under cold running water. When cool, drain well and pat dry. Cut into a fine julienne. Place in a nonreactive bowl, cover, and refrigerate until ready to use.

Peel jicama and cut into a fine julienne. Place in a nonreactive bowl, cover, and refrigerate until ready for use.

Whisk together orange juice, lemon juice, rice wine vinegar, peanut oil, sesame oil, orange rind, cayenne pepper, salt, and white pepper. When well combined, pour one-third of the mixture over the beetroots, one-third over the mangetout, and the remaining one-third over the jicama.

Place lettuce leaves on a chilled round serving platter. Place a mound of beetroots at the twelve, three, six, and nine o'clock positions on the plate. Place a mound of mangetout between the twelve and three and six and nine positions, and a mound of jicama between the three and six and nine and twelve positions. Place chive blossoms in the centre and serve immediately.

38

Cook vinegar and sugar in a small saucepan over medium heat for about 3 minutes or until sugar has dissolved. Remove from heat and set aside.

Heat oils in a heavy frying pan over medium heat. When hot, add peppercorns and cook for about 4 minutes or until peppercorns begin to smoke. Immediately remove from heat, cover, and set aside.

Remove stems and seeds from chilles and cut into a fine julienne. When oil has cooled, strain into a small saucepan. Add chilles and ginger and place over high heat. Cook, stirring constantly, for about 30 seconds or until chille and ginger begin to brown. Immediately add vinegar mixture and bring to a boil. When boiling, remove from heat.

Combine cabbage, cucumber, daikon, carrots, and coriander in a nonreactive bowl. Pour on hot dressing and toss to coat. Serve at room temperature or chilled.

Szechuan Slaw

Serves 6 to 8.

120mL; 4 fl oz rice wine vinegar

140g; 5 oz caster sugar

60mL; 2 fl oz corn oil

1 tablespoon sesame oil (available in Asian markets)

1 teaspoon Szechuan peppercorns (available in Asian markets)

6 guajillo chilles (or other dried hot red chilles)

60g; 2 oz finely julienned fresh ginger

170g; 6 oz shredded Chinese cabbage

140g; 5 oz julienned cucumber

170g; 6 oz shredded daikon (or Chinese radish) (available in Asian markets)

170g; 6 oz grated carrots

60g; 2 oz chopped fresh coriander (optional)

Main **C**ourses:

Poultry, **F**ish and **S**hellfish, **M**eat, and **O**ther **D**ishes

Tandoori **C**hicken

Coconut **C**hicken with **O**range **R**ice

Chicken **K**apama

Chicken **B**erbere

Hacked **C**hicken

Turkey **M**olé

Breast of **D**uck with **L**ime **S**auce and **L**ime **C**hutney

Red **D**evil **Q**uail

Fried **F**ish **I**ndian-**S**tyle

Red **S**napper à la **V**era **C**ruz

Barbecued **S**almon with **L**emon **C**hille **B**utter

Tuna with **W**asabi **H**ollandaise and **L**otus **B**lossoms

Brazilian **F**ish **S**tew

Spiced **S**autéed **S**quid

Harbour **I**sland **C**onch **F**ritters

Thai Sautéed Beef with Chilles, Peppers, and Peanuts

Ropa Vieja

Moroccan Spiced Steak

Red Lamb

Bobotie

Special Roasted Pork with Mashed Breadfruit
and Sautéed Okra

Roast Loin of Veal with Green Apple Mustard Sauce
and Mustard-Baked Apples

Spicy Corn Cheddar Soufflé

Cheese Enchiladas with Red Chille Salsa

Chille Cheese Strata

Chilli

Maccheroni all'Arrabbiata

Red Chille Couscous

Ants Climbing a Tree

Curry

Tandoori Chicken

Serves 6.

Real Tandoori Chicken is baked in a tandoor, the traditional clay oven of India, but this is a great approximation of the real thing. I do not add the food colouring that gives authentic Tandoori Chicken its bright orange colour. If you choose to do so, brush orange food colouring on the chicken pieces before marinating.

4 chicken legs

4 chicken thighs

4 chicken breasts, quartered (or any combination of chicken pieces you desire)

2 tablespoons fresh lemon juice

Salt (to taste)

600g; 1¼ lb plain yoghurt

2 tablespoons lime juice

140g; 5 oz chopped onion

1 tablespoon minced fresh ginger

1 teaspoon minced garlic

½ fresh hot red chille, seeded and chopped

1 tablespoon paprika

2 teaspoons Garam Masala (see page 13)

1 teaspoon turmeric

Using a small boning knife, make slits on both sides of the legs and thighs and the meaty side of the breasts. The slits should be about 4cm; 1½ inches long and run into the bone. Rub the chicken pieces with lemon juice. Place in a nonreactive container and set aside.

Process remaining ingredients in a blender or food processor fitted with the metal blade. Pour over the chicken and toss to coat well. Cover and refrigerate for at least 8 hours.

Preheat oven to Gas mark 9; 250°C; 500°F.

Place racks on baking sheets with sides. Lay chicken pieces on racks at least 2.5cm; 1 inch apart and immediately place in preheated oven. Bake for 20 minutes or until chicken is golden (or bright orange-brown if using food colouring). Serve immediately.

Coconut Chicken with Orange Rice

Serves 6.

Many flavours combine to make this one of my favourite chicken dishes.

2 tablespoons rapeseed oil

6 boneless, skinless, chicken breasts, halved

85 g; 3 oz chopped onion

2 tablespoons minced garlic

1 tablespoon minced fresh ginger

1 tablespoon minced shallots

30 g; 1 oz chopped macadamia nuts

1 whole habañero chille pepper, stemmed and seeded (or to taste)

½ teaspoon grated lemon rind

½ teaspoon grated orange rind

60mL; 2 fl oz Chille Oil (see page 12)

1 teaspoon soft brown sugar

1 teaspoon ground coriander

⅛ teaspoon ground turmeric

600mL; 1 pt Coconut Milk (see page 114)

2 stalks lemongrass (available in Asian markets)

Salt (to taste)

Orange Rice

45 g; 1½ oz chopped spring onion

30 g; 1 oz chopped, toasted macadamia nuts

Heat oil in a heavy frying pan over medium-high heat. When hot, fry chicken, turning frequently, for about 4 minutes or until lightly browned on all sides. Remove from heat and drain chicken on paper towels. Do not discard fat.

Process onion, garlic, ginger, shallots, nuts, chille, lemon and orange rinds, Chille Oil, brown sugar, and spices in a food processor fitted with the metal blade until well combined. Add 240mL; 8 fl oz Coconut Milk and process until smooth.

Return frying pan to medium heat. When hot, scrape onion mixture into the pan and cook, stirring constantly, for 2 minutes or until the mixture begins to color. Add browned chicken pieces, lemongrass, remaining Coconut Milk, and salt. Bring to a boil. When boiling, cover and lower heat to a simmer. Simmer for 30 minutes or until chicken is very tender and sauce is thick.

Place Orange Rice in the centre of a warm platter and surround it with chicken breasts. Discard lemongrass stalks and pour sauce over chicken. Sprinkle rice with spring onions and chicken with toasted nuts. Serve immediately.

Orange Rice

Serves 6.

350 g; 12 oz basmati rice

½ teaspoon saffron threads

180mL; 6 fl oz water

15 g; ½ oz butter or vegetable oil

85 g; 3 oz minced onion

1 teaspoon grated orange rind

¼ teaspoon ground turmeric

500mL; 16 fl oz hot chicken stock

2 large pieces dried orange peel (available in Asian markets)

Salt (to taste)

43

Rinse rice. Drain well and set aside.

Crumble saffron into water and set aside.

Melt butter in a medium-size frying pan over medium-high heat. When melted, add onion, orange rind, and turmeric. Sauté for about 3 minutes or until just soft. Add rice and sauté for about 5 minutes, or until rice is glistening and has absorbed the butter. Pour in chicken stock. Stir to combine. Add dried orange peel and salt. Bring to a boil.

When boiling, lower heat to a simmer and add saffron water. Cover and cook for about 25 minutes or until rice is just cooked and fluffy. Remove orange peel and serve hot.

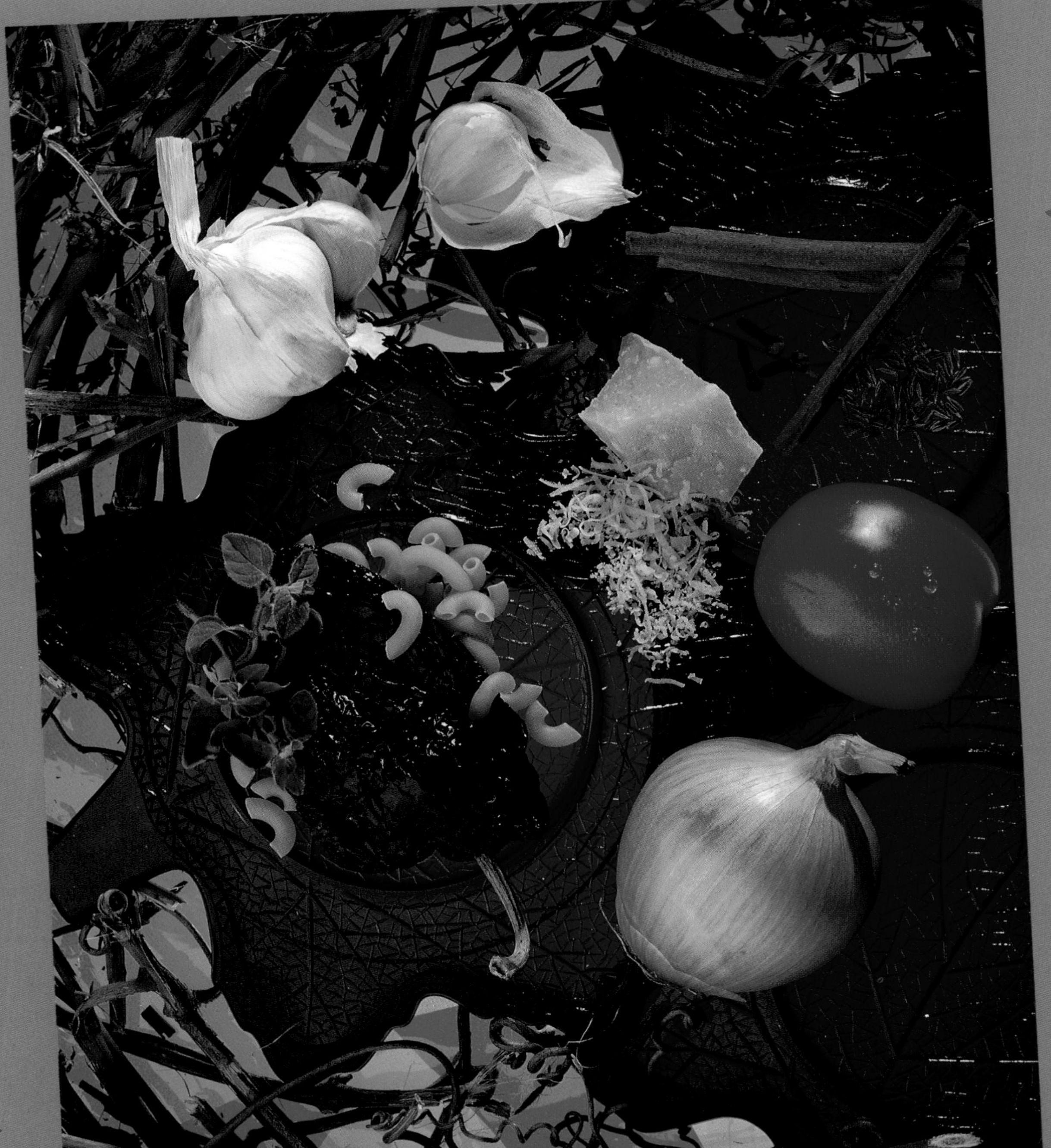

Chicken Kapama

Serves 6.

This traditional Greek recipe is wonderfully aromatic. It is a perfect buffet dish.

1 2 to 2.3kg; 4 to 5 lb chicken, cut into serving pieces

Juice of 1 lemon

1 teaspoon ground cumin

Salt (to taste)

Pepper (to taste)

60g; 2 oz butter

3 tablespoons olive oil

350g; 12 oz minced onion

3 tablespoons minced garlic

120mL; 4 fl oz retsina (or other dry white wine)

800g; 28 oz canned Italian plum tomatoes

180mL; 6 fl oz tomato paste

1 teaspoon minced fresh oregano

½ ancho chille (or other dried chille)

3 5cm; 2-inch cinnamon sticks

2 whole cloves

1 teaspoon light soft brown sugar

250mL; 8 fl oz water

450g; 1 lb elbow macaroni

30g; 1 oz browned butter (see Note, below)

3 tablespoons grated Kefalotyri cheese, or other dry hard cheese (available in Middle Eastern or Greek markets)

Wash and dry chicken, and rub with lemon juice. Generously coat chicken with cumin, salt, and pepper. Place in a casserole and set aside for 30 minutes.

Melt butter and oil in a heavy frying pan over medium heat. When hot, add chicken pieces a few at a time. Fry for about 3 minutes per side or until brown. When brown, return to casserole. When all chicken has been browned, add onion and garlic to frying pan and cook for 5 minutes or until just brown. Add retsina and cook to release all brown bits from the bottom of the pan. Scrape into casserole. Add tomatoes and tomato paste to chicken. Place casserole over medium heat.

Tie oregano, chille, cinnamon sticks, and cloves in a muslin bag and add to casserole. Stir in brown sugar and water. Raise heat and bring to a boil. When boiling, lower heat, cover, and simmer for about 40 minutes or until chicken is tender and sauce is thick.

A few minutes before chicken is done, cook elbow macaroni according to package directions. When macaroni is al dente, drain well and pour onto a serving platter. Pour browned butter all over the chicken and toss to mix. Place chicken pieces around the edge of the platter. Discard muslin bag and pour sauce over macaroni. Sprinkle with grated cheese and serve immediately.

Note: To brown butter, place in a small saucepan and cook over medium heat until butter takes on a rich, golden colour. Do not let it go brown or it will taste burned.

Chicken Berbere

Serves 6.

This method of cooking chicken is indigenous to Ethiopia.

2kg; 4 lb chicken pieces (breast, thighs, legs, wings)

1 tablespoon turmeric

1 tablespoon mustard seeds

2 teaspoons coriander seeds

1 teaspoon cardamon seeds

1 5cm; 2-inch cinnamon stick

1 teaspoon ground nutmeg

1 teaspoon ground allspice

1 teaspoon fenugreek seeds

70g; 2½ oz paprika

2 tablespoons cayenne pepper

1 teaspoon cracked black pepper

1 dried hot red chille of choice

2 pieces dried orange peel (available in Asian markets)

Salt (to taste)

1 tablespoon minced fresh ginger

120mL; 4 fl oz white wine

60mL; 2 fl oz corn oil

60mL; 2 fl oz fresh orange juice

3 limes, cut into quarters

Rinse chicken. Pat dry and set aside.

Place all spices, chille, orange peel, and salt in a medium-size frying pan over low heat. Cook, stirring constantly, for 5 minutes or until light brown and aromatic. Remove from heat and grind in a spice grinder until very fine. Return to frying pan over low heat. Add ginger, wine, oil, and orange juice. Cook, stirring constantly, for 3 minutes. Remove from heat and allow to come to room temperature.

Immediately rub each chicken with spice mixture. Place on a tray, cover, and refrigerate for at least 4 hours.

Preheat grill or barbecue.

Place chicken pieces under preheated grill (or on barbecue) and cook, turning frequently, for about 20 minutes or until meat is cooked and skin is crisp. Serve immediately with lime quarters.

Hacked Chicken

Serves 6.

This is based on a traditional Chinese recipe.

3 whole boneless, skinless, chicken breasts

1L; 32 fl oz chicken broth

1 small onion stuck with 2 cloves

½ ancho chille

1 stalk celery, washed and trimmed

1 carrot, washed and trimmed

120mL; 4 fl oz sesame paste (available in Asian markets)

60mL; 2 fl oz soy sauce

3 tablespoons rice wine vinegar (available in Asian markets)

3 tablespoons sesame oil (available in Asian markets)

2 tablespoons peanut butter

2 tablespoons chille paste (available in Asian markets)

2 teaspoons light soft brown sugar

60 g; 2 oz chopped spring onion, including some green

1 tablespoon minced fresh ginger

2 teaspoons minced garlic

1 tablespoon vegetable oil

700g; 1½ lb fresh spinach, washed, dried, and well trimmed

60g; 2 oz toasted sesame seeds

Cut chicken breasts in half. Rinse and pat dry. In a medium saucepan place chicken breasts in chicken broth seasoned with onion stuck with cloves, chille, celery, and carrot. Bring to a boil over high heat. When boiling, lower heat and simmer for about 15 minutes or until chicken is firm. Remove from heat and allow chicken to cool in broth. When cool, remove and pat dry. Using your fingers, pull chicken meat off in long strips. Set aside. Reserve broth for another use.

Combine sesame paste, soy sauce, rice wine vinegar, 2 tablespoons sesame oil, peanut butter, chille paste, brown sugar, spring onion, ginger, and garlic in a nonreactive bowl. Stir to blend well. Add a bit of chicken stock if sauce is too thick.

Heat remaining sesame oil and vegetable oil in a wok. When hot, add spinach and quickly stir-fry so the leaves are slightly wilted. Place spinach on a serving platter. Place chicken in the centre. Pour sesame over chicken. Sprinkle with toasted sesame seeds and serve immediately.

Turkey Molé

Serves 6.

In Mexico, molé simply means chille sauce. However, outside Mexico it has come to signify a chille sauce flavoured with unsweetened chocolate. This sensational sauce can also be used with chicken or pork.

2.3kg; 5 lb turkey parts (legs, breasts, thighs)

60mL; 2 fl oz vegetable oil

700mL; 24 fl oz chicken stock

700mL; 24 fl oz water

Salt (to taste)

Pepper (to taste)

6 ancho chilles

4 mulato chilles

6 chipotle chilles

255g; 9 oz chopped red onion

285g; 10 oz chopped, peeled, seedless tomatoes

2 cloves garlic, peeled and chopped

170g; 6 oz blanched almonds

60g; 2 oz toasted sesame seeds

½ teaspoon ground coriander

½ teaspoon ground cinnamon

½ teaspoon ground anise

Pinch cloves

1 corn tortilla, quartered

30g; 1 oz unsweetened chocolate

1 tablespoon pure maple syrup (optional)

170g; 6 oz chopped avocado

1 teaspoon fresh lime juice

Wash turkey parts and pat dry. Heat 2 tablespoons oil in a heavy frying pan over medium heat. When hot, add turkey and fry, turning frequently, for about 5 minutes or until turkey is well browned. Place browned turkey in a heavy saucepan. Add stock, water, salt, and pepper. Place over medium heat and bring to a boil. Lower heat and simmer for about hour or until turkey has just cooked through. Drain, reserving broth. Set turkey aside to cool.

Cut chilles into pieces and place in hot water to just cover for about 30 minutes or until soft. Pour into a blender with the onion, 140g; 5 oz tomatoes, and garlic. Process until smooth. Add almonds, 2 tablespoons sesame seeds, spices, and tortilla quarters, and process until it is a coarse paste.

Heat remaining oil in a heavy frying pan over medium heat. When hot, add chille paste and sauté, stirring constantly, for 3 minutes. Stir in 500mL; 16 fl oz turkey broth and cook for about 3 minutes or until hot. Add chocolate and cook, stirring constantly, for about 5 minutes or until chocolate has melted and sauce is thick. Taste and adjust seasonings with salt and pepper. You may add maple syrup if sauce needs sweetening.

Preheat oven to Gas mark 4; 180°C; 350°F.

Pull turkey from skin and bones. Lay meat in bottom of a 2L; 64 fl oz casserole. Pour sauce over the top, cover, and bake for about 20 minutes or until flavours are well combined. Remove from oven, uncover, and sprinkle top with sesame seeds. Keep warm.

Combine avocado, remaining tomatoes, and lime juice, and season with salt and pepper. Garnish edges of casserole with avocado mixture and serve.

Breast of Duck with Lime Sauce and Lime Chutney

Serves 6.

This is quite a formal presentation, worthy of the most festive occasion.

3 whole boneless duck breasts

60mL; 2 fl oz Chartreuse

2 tablespoons rapeseed oil

1 teaspoon grated lime rind

Salt (to taste)

Pepper (to taste)

60g; 2 oz unsalted butter

120mL; 4 fl oz Riesling or other light white wine

80mL; 2½ fl oz duck or beef stock

60mL; 2 fl oz fresh lime juice

3 teaspoons champagne vinegar

60mL; 2 fl oz lime blossom honey

1 tablespoon minced fresh ginger

1 5cm; 2-inch cinnamon stick

½ teaspoon minced fresh sage

Lime Chutney

Trim skin and fat from duck breasts. Cut in half. Combine Chartreuse, oil, lime rind, salt, and pepper. Generously coat duck with mixture, cover, and set aside for 30 minutes.

Melt 30g; 1 oz butter in a heavy frying pan over medium heat. When hot, add duck. Cook for about 4 minutes per side or until outside is brown and duck is still rare. Do not burn. Remove from pan and keep warm.

Add wine, stock, lime juice, champagne vinegar, honey, ginger, cinnamon stick, and sage to frying pan. Cook, stirring constantly, for about 5 minutes or until sauce is reduced to about 180mL; 6 fl oz. Remove from heat and press through a fine sieve. Return any juices from the resting duck to the pan. Bring to a boil. Lower heat and whisk in remaining butter a bit at a time until well combined.

Slice the duck breasts on the diagonal. Slightly fan each one out on a serving platter and coat with sauce. Garnish platter with Lime Chutney and serve immediately.

Lime Chutney

Makes approximately 1L; 32 fl oz.

85g; 3 oz seeded and chopped whole limes

30g; 1 oz seeded and chopped whole oranges

170g; 6 oz cored and chopped tart green apples (such as Granny Smith)

85g; 3 oz golden raisins

¼ chopped onion

1 tablespoon minced garlic

1 teaspoon minced fresh ginger

1 teaspoon minced fresh hot green chille

½ teaspoon mustard seed

170g; 6 oz light soft brown sugar

180mL; 6 fl oz tequila

85g; 3 oz toasted unsalted sunflower seeds

Combine all the ingredients except sunflower seeds in a heavy saucepan over medium heat. Bring to a boil. Lower heat and simmer for 1 hour. Remove from heat and allow to cool slightly. Stir in sunflower seeds. Store, covered and refrigerated, until ready to use. The chutney may be refrigerated for up to 3 months.

49

Fried Fish Indian-Style

Serves 6.

2 teaspoons ground cumin

1 teaspoon ground turmeric

½ teaspoon Curry Powder (see page 13)

½ teaspoon cayenne pepper

½ teaspoon ground pepper

¼ teaspoon salt (or to taste)

6 large, boneless, firm whitefish fillets (sole, flounder, etc.)

230g; 8 oz plain yoghurt

1 egg (size 3)

1 tablespoon lemon juice

140g; 5 oz extra-fine bread crumbs

3 tablespoons minced fresh coriander

45g; 1½ oz butter

80mL; 2½ fl oz vegetable oil

1 lemon or lime, cut into wedges

Red Devil Quail

Serves 6.

This is based on a traditional Indonesian method of cooking chicken. Any poultry, game or meat can be barbecued in this fashion.

6 whole quail

Juice of 1 lemon

1 tablespoon tamarind (available in Asian markets) dissolved in 2 tablespoons warm water

250mL; 8 fl oz Coconut Milk (see page 114)

45g; 1½ oz chopped onion

2 fresh hot red or green chilles, stemmed and seeded

1 tablespoon minced garlic

Salt (to taste)

Preheat grill or barbecue.

Split quail in half lengthwise. Rub with lemon juice. Place on grill pan in grill or on the barbecue and grill for 2 minutes per side. Remove from grill and set aside. Do not turn off grill or barbecue.

Strain tamarind through fine sieve. Combine with Coconut Milk, onion, chille, garlic, and salt. Place in blender and process until smooth.

Using a cleaver, lightly pound each quail half to slightly flatten. Place in a heavy, non-stick fry pan over medium heat. Pour sauce over quail and fry, stirring frequently, for about 6 minutes or until quail has absorbed most of the sauce. Return quail to grill. Brush skin side with any remaining sauce and grill, skin side up (or barbecue skin side down), for about 2 minutes or until crisp. Serve immediately.

Combine spices and salt. Sprinkle on both sides of the fish fillets and let set for 10 minutes.

Combine yoghurt, egg, and lemon juice in a shallow bowl. Set aside.

Combine bread crumbs and coriander in a shallow dish. Dip seasoned fillets into yoghurt mixture, then into bread crumbs, making sure that bread crumbs adhere to fillets. If there are any bare spots, brush with yoghurt mixture and pat in some bread crumbs.

Heat butter and oil in a heavy frying pan over medium heat. When hot, add fillets a few at a time, and fry for about 3 minutes per side or until fish is flaky and the outside is crisp. Drain on a paper towel and serve immediately with lemon or lime wedges.

Red Snapper à la Vera Cruz

Serves 6.

This is perhaps the most well-known Mexican fish dish. Its sauce can, of course, be used with any firm-fleshed fish.

1.5kg; 3 lb well-trimmed red snapper fillets (or 1 large, cleaned red snapper, head and bones removed)

2 tablespoons fresh lime juice

Salt (to taste)

Pepper (to taste)

18 very small new potatoes

1kg; 42 oz chopped canned Italian plum tomatoes

1 tablespoon vegetable oil

170g; 6 oz finely chopped onion

130g; 4½ oz chopped red pepper

1 tablespoon minced garlic

3 tablespoons well-drained capers

1 serrano chille, stemmed, seeded, and chopped

170g; 6 oz well-drained, small pimento-stuffed olives

30g; 1 oz chopped fresh parsley or coriander

Season fish with lime juice, salt, and pepper. Set aside to marinate for about 15 minutes.

Place potatoes in cold water to cover in a medium-size saucepan over medium heat. Bring to a boil. When boiling, lower heat and simmer for about 15 minutes or until well done. Drain and keep warm.

Puree tomatoes in a food processor fitted with the metal blade. Set aside.

Heat oil in a heavy frying pan over medium heat. When hot, add the onion, pepper, and garlic. Cook, stirring frequently, for about 4 minutes or until soft. Add tomatoes, capers, chille, and olives. Stir to blend. When well blended, add the fish, covering the top of the fish with some of the sauce. Bring to a simmer over medium heat. Lower heat and cook for about 6 minutes or until fish is cooked through. Remove fish and keep warm. If sauce is too thin, raise heat and reduce until thick.

Place fish on a warm serving platter. Coat with sauce. Arrange potatoes around the edge and serve immediately.

Preheat grill or barbecue.

Use half of the onion mixture to coat one side of each of the salmon steaks. Place under preheated grill (or on barbecue) and cook for about 4 minutes. Turn, and use remaining onion mixture to coat uncooked side. Return to the grill or barbecue and cook for about 4 minutes or until salmon is just cooked through. Serve immediately, dressed with Lemon Chille Butter.

Lemon Chille Butter

Makes approximately 115g; 4 oz.

115g; 4 oz unsalted butter

1 tablespoon dried red pepper flakes

1 tablespoon fresh lemon juice

Melt butter in a small saucepan over low heat. Remove from heat and add red pepper flakes; allow to stand for at least 1 hour, keeping warm.

Strain butter into a small frying pan. Discard red pepper flakes. Heat butter over medium heat until golden brown. Remove from heat and stir in lemon juice. Keep warm until ready to serve.

Barbecued Salmon with Lemon Chille Butter

Serves 6.

This is a refreshing way to add zest to plain barbecued salmon.

6 230g; 8 oz salmon steaks or salmon fillets

2 tablespoons fresh lemon juice

45g; 1½ oz chopped onion

1 tablespoon chopped garlic

1 tablespoon chopped fresh parsley

1 tablespoon grated lemon rind

1 teaspoon chopped fresh dill

60mL; 2 fl oz rapeseed oil

1½ teaspoons paprika

1½ teaspoons ground white pepper

⅛ teaspoon cayenne pepper

Salt (to taste)

Lemon Chille Butter

Rub salmon with lemon juice. Set aside.

Process onion, garlic, parsley, lemon rind, dill, oil, paprika, white and cayenne peppers, and salt in a blender or a food processor fitted with the metal blade, until well combined and quite thick. If too thick, add extra lemon juice a bit at a time.

Tuna with Wasabi Hollandaise and Lotus Blossoms

Serves 6.

120mL; 4 fl oz sake

120mL; 4 fl oz soy sauce

2 tablespoons peanut oil

½ teaspoon cayenne pepper

6 200g; 7-oz, 2.5cm; 1-inch-thick tuna steaks

Lotus Blossoms

115g; 4 oz pickled ginger (available in Asian markets)

Wasabi Hollandaise

Combine sake, soy sauce, oil, and cayenne pepper. Rub tuna with this mixture and set aside.

Preheat grill or barbecue.

Place tuna steaks under preheated grill (or on barbecue) and cook for 3 minutes per side for medium rare. Place on a warm serving platter. Garnish with Lotus Blossoms, pickled ginger, and drizzle with Wasabi Hollandaise. Serve remaining hollandaise on the side.

Lotus Blossoms

Serves 6.

1 canned lotus root (available in Asian markets)

1 egg, separated (size 3)

60mL; 2 fl oz water

Approximately 1L; 32 fl oz vegetable oil

70g; 2½ oz plain flour

1 tablespoon cornflour

1 teaspoon baking powder

Salt (to taste)

Drain the lotus root and cut, crosswise, into 0.5cm; ¼-inch slices. Trim around the holes into the outer edge to make a flower shape out of each slice. You can make as many as the root allows, but you should allow at least 2 per person.

Beat egg yolk and water together. Whisk in 1 teaspoon of oil.

Combine flour, cornflour, baking powder, and salt, then whisk into the egg. Beat egg white until stiff, then fold into the batter.

Heat remaining oil in deep-fry pan to 185°C; 365°F on a food thermometer. Dip lotus root into batter, shaking off excess, then gently slide into the hot oil a few at a time. Fry for about 1 minute or until golden. Remove from oil and drain on paper towels. Serve hot or at room temperature.

Wasabi Hollandaise

Makes approximately 300mL; 10 fl oz.

1 tablespoon wasabi powder (available in Asian markets)

1 tablespoon water

2 tablespoons grated fresh ginger

230g; 8 oz melted unsalted butter, kept warm

3 egg yolks (size 3)

1 tablespoon fresh lemon juice

2 teaspoons fresh orange juice

¼ teaspoon salt

Pinch cayenne pepper

Blend wasabi powder with 1 tablespoon water until it makes a smooth paste. Set aside.

Press ginger through a fine sieve, reserving the juice and discarding the solids.

Combine wasabi paste, ginger juice, melted butter, egg yolks, lemon and orange juices, salt, and cayenne pepper in a blender or a food processor fitted with the metal blade. Combine, using quick on-and-off turns. Do not overmix. Remove from blender or processor bowl and place in a container that can be used in a microwave oven. Cook in the microwave on medium-high for 1 minute. Remove from microwave and whisk vigorously. (The sauce may appear curdled, but the whisking will make it smooth.) If sauce is runny, return to microwave and cook for an additional 30 seconds at medium. Whisk until smooth. Keep warm over warm water until ready to use.

Brazilian Fish Stew

Serves 6.

This stew, like many Brazilian dishes, is enhanced by the flavour and colour of the traditional *dendé* (palm oil). If it is not available to you, simply use any vegetable or fruit oil.

1kg; 2½ lb boneless fillets of any firm whitefish

230g; ½ lb small prawns, peeled, deveined, and tails removed

700g; 1½ lb peeled and chopped fresh tomatoes

350g; 12 oz chopped onion

15g; ½ oz chopped fresh coriander

1 tablespoon minced garlic

1 serrano chille, stemmed, seeded, and chopped

60mL; 2 fl oz fresh lime juice

3 tablespoons dendé oil (available in Latin and South American markets)

Salt (to taste)

Pepper (to taste)

1 red pepper, stemmed, seeded, and diced

1 green pepper, stemmed, seeded, and diced

120mL; 4 fl oz fish stock or water

Cut the fillets into bite-size pieces. Cut the prawns in half lengthwise. Place in a shallow, nonreactive bowl and set aside.

Combine the tomatoes, onion, coriander, garlic, chille, lime juice, dendé oil, salt, and pepper in a food processor fitted with the metal blade. Process until smooth. Pour over fish and allow to marinate for 1 hour.

Place marinated fish in a heavy saucepan over medium heat. Add peppers and fish stock. Bring to a boil. Lower heat and simmer for about 10 minutes or until fish is cooked through. Serve immediately with rice, if desired.

54

Spiced Sautéed Squid

Serves 6.

This is my version of a Southeast Asian squid dish.

900g; 2 lb fresh squid, cleaned and cut into 1cm; ½-inch rings

2 tablespoons fresh lime juice

Salt (to taste)

Pepper (to taste)

3 tablespoons light soft brown sugar

3 tablespoons soy sauce

¼ teaspoon ground star anise

1 tablespoon water

60mL; 2 fl oz peanut oil

30g; 1 oz thinly sliced onion

2 tablespoons sliced garlic

115g; 4 oz peeled, seeded, and diced tomatoes

60g; 2 oz roasted unsalted peanuts

¼ teaspoon cayenne pepper

Pinch ground cloves

Pinch ground cinnamon

Pinch ground nutmeg

Toss squid with lime juice, salt, and pepper and set aside.

Melt sugar in a small saucepan over medium heat. When melted, add soy sauce, star anise, and water and cook for 10 minutes or until slightly thickened. Set aside.

Heat oil in a wok over medium-high heat. When hot, add squid and stir-fry for 3 minutes or until squid has set. Remove squid and keep warm.

Add onion and garlic to wok and stir-fry for 3 minutes or until just beginning to brown. Add squid, soy sauce mixture, and remaining ingredients and cook, stirring constantly, for about 5 minutes or until sauce has begun to thicken. Taste and adjust seasonings with salt and pepper, if necessary. Serve immediately.

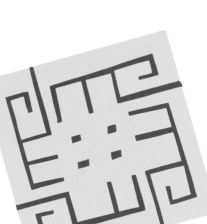

Harbour Island Conch Fritters

Serves 6.

Sitting on the beach of Harbour Island in the Bahamas or on the bay side watching the sunset, eating conch fritters and drinking daiquiris, is surely heaven on earth. Throughout the Bahamas these fritters are eaten as a snack, but I find them too filling to be followed by a meal. So I serve them as an entrée.

700g; 1½ lb conch

45g; 1½ oz minced onion

45g; 1½ oz minced celery

2 tablespoons minced red pepper

2 tablespoons minced green pepper

1 habañero chille, stemmed and seeded (or to taste)

1 teaspoon minced fresh thyme

1 teaspoon minced fresh parsley

Pinch ground sage

500g; 18 oz plain flour

2 teaspoons baking powder

Salt (to taste)

Pepper (to taste)

Approximately 1.2L; 2 pt vegetable oil

2 lemons or limes, cut into wedges

Pound the conch with a mallet or cleaver until quite tender. Cut into pieces and place in a food processor fitted with the metal blade. Process, using quick on-and-off turns, until coarsely chopped. Add onion, celery, peppers, chille, thyme, parsley, and sage to food processor bowl. Combine using quick on-and-off turns. Pour into a large bowl and stir in 2 tablespoons oil.

Combine flour, baking powder, salt, and pepper. Stir into conch mixture. Add water, 1 tablespoon at a time, to make a stiff batter.

Heat remaining oil to 185°C; 360°F on a food thermometer in a deep-fry pan. When hot, drop in fritter batter by the tablespoonful a few at a time. Fry for about 4 minutes or until crisp, golden, and cooked through. Serve hot with lemon or lime wedges and Hot Sauce (see page 12) or any spicy sauce or salsa on the side.

57

Thai Sautéed Beef with Chilles, Peppers, and Peanuts

Serves 6.

6 dried hot red chilles

3 green peppers

2 bunches spring onions

700g; 1½ lb lean fillet of beef

3 tablespoons minced fresh ginger

3 tablespoons minced shallots

3 tablespoons minced fresh coriander

2 tablespoons minced garlic

1 tablespoon minced lemongrass (available in Asian markets)

1 tablespoon minced fresh basil

355mL; 12 fl oz Coconut Milk (see page 114)

3 tablespoons rice wine (available in Asian markets)

2 tablespoons soy sauce

1 tablespoon Thai fish sauce (available in Asian markets)

1 tablespoon fresh lime juice

1 tablespoon cornflour

1 tablespoon peanut oil

130g; 4½ oz roasted unsalted peanuts

1 teaspoon light soft brown sugar

2 tablespoons shredded basil leaves (optional)

2 tablespoons shredded hot red chilles (optional)

Place dried chilles in boiling water to cover for 30 minutes or until soft. When soft, drain and stem. Set aside.

Wash, core, and seed peppers. Remove all white membrane and cut into thin slices. Set aside.

Wash and trim spring onions. Cut into 0.5cm; ¼-inch pieces using some of the green part. Set aside.

Cut beef into thin strips. Place in a nonreactive container and set aside.

Combine dried chilles, ginger, shallots, coriander, garlic, lemongrass, basil, Coconut Milk, rice wine, soy and fish sauces, and lime juice in a blender. Combine until smooth, then pour over beef. Cover and marinate for 1 hour. Drain, reserving marinade. Add cornflour to marinade and set aside.

Heat oil in a wok over medium-high heat. When hot, add beef and stir-fry for about 3 minutes or until just brown. Remove and place on paper towels to drain. Add green pepper and spring onion to wok and stir-fry for 2 minutes. Add beef, peanuts, and brown sugar, and continue to stir-fry for 2 minutes. Raise heat to high and add reserved marinade. Stir-fry for 2 minutes or until well glazed. Pour onto a serving platter and garnish with shredded basil leaves and chilles, if desired.

Ropa Vieja

Serves 6.

This is one of my favourite Cuban dishes, taught to me by Maria Incarnacion Conception de Cespedes. Ropa Vieja means "old clothes," from the ragged look of the shredded meat. It is delicious.

1.6kg; 3½ lb very lean flank steak

230g; 8 oz diced onion

140g; 5 oz diced carrots

60g; 2 oz diced leeks

1 tablespoon minced fresh parsley

1 tablespoon tomato paste

500mL; 16 fl oz beef broth

2 tablespoons peanut oil

115g; 4 oz diced red pepper

115g; 4 oz diced green pepper

1 fresh, hot, red chille, stemmed and chopped (or to taste)

1 tablespoon minced garlic

570g; 20 oz chopped canned Italian plum tomatoes

1 5cm; 2-inch cinnamon stick

¼ teaspoon ground cloves

1 bay leaf

1 sprig fresh thyme

60g; 2 oz diced canned pimentos

Place steak, 115g; 4 oz of onion, carrots, leeks, parsley, tomato paste, and beef broth in a heavy saucepan. Add enough water to cover. Stir to combine. Place over medium heat and bring to a boil. Lower heat, cover, and simmer for about 1½ hours or until meat is very tender. Remove from heat and allow to cool in the broth. When cool, remove meat and pull it apart into thin shreds. Set aside.

Strain the broth, reserving the liquid and discarding the solids. Heat oil in a heavy frying pan over medium-high heat. When hot, add the remaining onion, peppers, chille, and garlic. Fry, stirring frequently, for about 5 minutes or until vegetables are quite soft. Add tomatoes, 250mL; 8 fl oz of reserved broth, spices, and herbs and cook for about 30 minutes or until sauce is very thick. Add the reserved steak, pimentos, and 250mL; 8 fl oz of reserved broth. Stir to heat through. Remove cinnamon stick and thyme sprig. Serve hot with white rice and black beans, if desired.

Moroccan Spiced Steak

Serves 6.

1 1.6kg; 3½-lb well-trimmed flank steak

4 cloves garlic, peeled and halved

180mL; 6 fl oz olive oil

60mL; 2 fl oz fresh lemon juice

2 tablespoons pomegranate juice (or cranberry juice)

2 teaspoons sherry

170g; 6 oz chopped onion

85g; 3 oz chopped canned Italian plum tomatoes

2 tablespoons minced fresh parsley

1 tablespoon grated fresh ginger

1 teaspoon minced fresh oregano

3 seedless dried, chopped prunes

1 tablespoon ground cumin

1 tablespoon ground chille powder

1 teaspoon ground cinnamon

1½ teaspoons cracked black pepper

¼ teaspoon saffron threads

½ teaspoon salt (or to taste)

Make 8 small incisions in each side of the steak. Insert a garlic half into each incision.

Combine remaining ingredients in a nonreactive, shallow dish large enough to hold the steak. Add steak. Cover and refrigerate for 1 hour. Uncover and turn steak. Rewrap and refrigerate for at least 4 hours, turning occasionally.

Preheat grill or barbecue. When hot, remove the steak from the marinade and place on a grill rack or barbecue. Place under preheated grill (or barbecue) and cook for about 4 minutes per side for medium-rare.

Place the remaining marinade in a blender and process until smooth. Pour into a small saucepan over medium heat. Cook, stirring frequently, for about 5 minutes or until flavours are well combined and sauce has thickened slightly.

Cut steaks on the bias into thin strips. Place on a warm platter and drizzle with sauce. Serve warm with remaining sauce on the side.

Red Lamb

Serves 4 to 6.

This Indian recipe was the star at a benefit for the opening of the New York City Fire Museum.

60mL; 2 fl oz rapeseed oil

900g; 2 lb very lean lamb stew meat, cut into 4cm; 1½-inch cubes

340g; 12 oz chopped onion

2 tablespoons minced garlic

½ teaspoon whole peppercorns

6 whole cloves

6 cardamon pods

1 5cm; 2-inch cinnamon stick

1 bay leaf

60g; 2 oz chopped fresh ginger

2 serrano chilles, stemmed (or to taste)

120 mL; 4 fl oz water

2 teaspoons ground cumin

1 teaspoon ground coriander

¾ teaspoon cayenne pepper

¼ teaspoon red pepper flakes (or to taste)

Salt (to taste)

Black pepper (to taste)

350g; 12 oz plain yoghurt

570g; 20 oz chopped, skinless, seedless, fresh tomatoes

355mL; 12 fl oz lamb stock or water

½ teaspoon Garam Masala (see page 13)

Heat 2 tablespoons oil in a heavy casserole over medium-high heat. When hot, add lamb in batches and sauté, stirring frequently, for about 5 minutes or until well browned on all sides. Remove from pan and drain on paper towels. Place meat on a plate and set aside.

Lower heat to medium and add remaining oil to casserole. When hot, add onion, garlic, peppercorns, cloves, cardamon, cinnamon stick, and bay leaf. Cook, stirring constantly, for 5 minutes or until onions begin to brown. Puree ginger, chilles, and water in a blender and add to the browned onions. Stir to combine, then add lamb, cumin, coriander, cayenne pepper, red pepper flakes, salt, and pepper. Cook, stirring frequently, for 5 minutes. Then add yoghurt, 1 tablespoon at a time, until well blended.

Preheat oven to Gas mark 4; 180°C; 350°F.

Stir tomatoes and lamb stock or water into the lamb mixture. Cover and place in preheated oven. Bake for about 45 minutes or until lamb is very tender. Remove from oven. If the sauce is not thick, place over medium-high heat and bring to a boil. Boil, stirring constantly, until sauce has reduced. Stir in Garam Masala, taste, and adjust seasonings. Serve immediately.

61

Bobotie

Serves 6 to 8.

I'm told that there are many versions of this tasty lamb casserole. I was introduced to it by a Caribbean chef who had learned it in Africa.

3 tablespoons rapeseed oil

170g; 6 oz chopped onion

1 tablespoon minced serrano chille

900g; 2 lb very lean lamb, either ground or cut into a very fine dice

70g; 2½ oz chopped dried apricots

45g; 1½ oz yellow raisins

2 tablespoons Curry Powder (see page 13)

½ teaspoon ground cumin

140g; 5 oz chopped canned Italian plum tomatoes

2 tablespoons apricot or peach jam

120mL; 4 fl oz fresh lemon juice

60mL; 2 fl oz fresh orange juice

85g; 3 oz slivered blanched almonds

650mL; 22 fl oz double cream

4 eggs (size 3)

¼ teaspoon grated fresh nutmeg

Salt (to taste)

Pepper (to taste)

Heat oil in a heavy frying pan over medium heat. When hot, add onion, garlic, and chille and fry, stirring frequently, for about 3 minutes or until slightly soft. Add lamb and continue to cook, stirring frequently, for about 5 minutes or until lamb is beginning to brown. Stir in apricots, raisins, Curry Powder, cumin, tomatoes, jam, and lemon and orange juices. Continue to cook for 7 minutes or until pan is almost dry. Stir in almonds and 180mL; 6 fl oz heavy cream. Remove from heat and allow to cool.

Preheat oven to Gas mark 4; 180°C; 350°F.

Scrape lamb into a 2L; 64 fl oz casserole. Whisk together remaining ingredients. When well combined, pour over meat in casserole. Place in preheated oven and bake for about 1 hour or until custard has set. Serve hot with rice, if desired.

Special Roasted Pork with Mashed Breadfruit and Sautéed Okra

Serves 6.

I have replaced the traditional fresh ham with the leaner loin of pork for my version of a wonderfully flavourful Caribbean roast.

1 1.8kg; 4 lb boneless loin of pork, tied

1 red pepper, cored, seeded, and chopped

170g; 6 oz minced onion

2 tablespoons minced garlic

2 tablespoons minced fresh parsley

2 tablespoons grated fresh ginger

1 tablespoon minced fresh chives

1 teaspoon minced habañero chille (or to taste)

1 teaspoon minced fresh thyme

1 teaspoon minced fresh marjoram

45g; 1½ oz dark raisins

60mL; 2 fl oz fresh lime juice

2 tablespoons soy sauce

2 tablespoons olive oil

60g; 2 oz dark soft brown sugar

Salt (to taste)

Pepper (to taste)

Mashed Breadfruit

Sautéed Okra

64

Place pork in a nonreactive bowl. Combine pepper, onion, garlic, parsley, ginger, chives, chille, herbs, raisins, lime juice, soy sauce, olive oil, sugar, salt, and pepper. When well combined, pour over pork. Cover and refrigerate for 6 hours, turning frequently.

Preheat oven to Gas mark 9; 240°C; 475°F.

Place pork with marinade into a roasting pan. Cover tightly and place in preheated oven. Roast for 15 minutes, then lower heat to Gas mark 5; 190°C; 375°F. Roast for about 1½ hours or until meat thermometer registers 73°C; 165°F when inserted into the centre of the roast. Five minutes before the meat is ready, place pork on a rack in a clean roasting pan. Raise heat to Gas mark 9½; 260°C; 500°F and allow outside to crisp.

Strain pan juices from roasting pan into a small saucepan. Place over medium heat and keep warm.

When pork is crisp, remove from oven and slice into serving-size pieces. Place on a warm serving platter. Serve with Mashed Breadfruit and drizzle all with pan juices. Serve Sautéed Okra on the side.

Mashed Breadfruit

Serves 6.

900g; 2 lb fresh breadfruit (available in Latin-American markets); canned may be substituted

250mL; 8 fl oz chicken stock

I clove garlic, peeled

Salt (to taste)

Pepper (to taste)

Approximately 80mL; 2½ fl oz double cream

45g; 1½ oz butter

Peel, core, and dice breadfruit. Place in a nonreactive bowl with cold water to cover for 1 hour. Drain well.

Place breadfruit in a medium-size saucepan with chicken stock, garlic, salt, pepper, and water to cover. Bring to a boil over medium-high heat. When boiling, lower heat and simmer for about 25 minutes or until breadfruit is soft. Drain well.

Place breadfruit in the bowl of an electric mixer. Add cream, butter, more salt and pepper, if desired, and beat until fluffy. Serve immediately.

Sautéed Okra

Serves 6.

700g; 1½ lb fresh okra

2 tablespoons olive oil

85g; 3 oz diced onion

½ minced fresh hot red chille (or to taste)

I tablespoon tomato paste

I teaspoon fresh lime juice

Salt (to taste)

Pepper (to taste)

Trim okra and cut into 1cm; ½-inch pieces.

Heat oil in a heavy frying pan over medium heat. When hot, add onion and chille and sauté for 3 minutes. Add okra and stir to combine. Lower heat, cover, and let cook for about 5 minutes or until okra is just soft. Add tomato paste, lime juice, salt, and pepper. Cook, stirring frequently, for about 5 minutes or until flavours are well combined and okra is tender but not gummy. Serve immediately.

Roast Loin of Veal with Green Apple Mustard Sauce and Mustard-Baked Apples

Serves 6.

1 1.5kg; 3½ lb boneless loin of veal

1 tablespoon vegetable oil

Salt (to taste)

Pepper (to taste)

120mL; 4 fl oz dry white wine

Green Apple Mustard Sauce

Mustard-Baked Apples

Preheat oven to Gas mark 8; 230°C; 450°F.

Season veal with oil, salt, and pepper. Place on a rack in a roasting pan. Add white wine and 250mL; 8 fl oz water to pan. Place in preheated oven and roast for about 1½ hours or until meat thermometer registers 71°C; 160°F for medium (or to the degree of doneness you desire). Remove from oven and allow to set for 10 minutes, keeping warm.

Slice meat and place on a warm platter. Drizzle with Green Apple Mustard Sauce and garnish with Mustard-Baked Apples.

Green Apple Mustard Sauce

Makes about 600mL; 1 pt.

60g; 2 oz butter

85g; 3 oz minced shallots

½ teaspoon minced serrano chille

4 tart green apples (such as Granny Smith), peeled, cored, and chopped

3 tablespoons Calvados or apple cider

2 tablespoons Dijon mustard

2 tablespoons honey mustard

½ teaspoon dry mustard

360mL; 12 fl oz double cream

1 tablespoon fresh lime juice

Salt (to taste)

White pepper (to taste)

Melt butter in a heavy saucepan over medium heat. When melted, add shallots and chille. Sauté, stirring frequently, for about 5 minutes or until shallots are very soft. Add apples and Calvados or apple cider. Lower heat. Cover and cook for about 10 minutes or until apples are tender. Stir in mustards and cream. Raise heat to medium and cook for about 8 minutes or until liquid has reduced and apples are mushy. Stir in lime juice, salt, and pepper. Remove from heat and pour into a blender. Process until smooth. Strain through a fine sieve. Keep warm over hot water until ready to serve.

Mustard-Baked Apples

Serves 6.

6 firm, tart green apples (such as Granny Smith)

1 tablespoon fresh lemon juice

230g; 8 oz butter

115g; 4 oz light soft brown sugar

3 tablespoons whole-grain mustard

1 teaspoon ground cinnamon

Dash nutmeg

Dash cloves

Dash cayenne pepper

1 tablespoon cinnamon dot sweets

½ teaspoon grated lemon rind

215g; 7½ oz extra-fine bread crumbs

1 teaspoon dry mustard

Salt (to taste)

Salt (to taste)

Peel and core apples. Cut crosswise into 0.5cm; ¼-inch slices. Place in a nonreactive bowl filled with cold water. Add lemon juice to keep apples from browning.

Combine butter, brown sugar, and whole-grain mustard in a small saucepan over medium heat. When sugar has melted, add spices, cinnamon dot sweets, and lemon rind. Cook, stirring frequently, until sweets have dissolved. Remove from heat and pour into a shallow dish. Keep warm.

Combine bread crumbs, dry mustard, and salt and place in a flat dish.

Preheat oven to Gas mark 6; 200°C; 400°F.

Generously grease a baking sheet. One at a time, dry apple slices. Dip into butter mixture, then into seasoned bread crumbs. Place on a prepared baking sheet. When baking sheet is filled, place in preheated oven and bake apples for about 10 minutes or until coating is lightly browned and apples are just beginning to cook. Serve immediately.

Spicy **C**orn **C**heddar **S**oufflé

Serves 6.

An old favourite with a little heat.

100g; 3½ oz butter

45g; 1½ oz plain flour

¼ teaspoon dry mustard

Pinch cayenne pepper

250mL; 8 fl oz warm milk

140g; 5 oz grated cheddar cheese

170g; 6 oz cooked sweetcorn

3 tablespoons finely diced red pepper

1 teaspoon minced fresh hot green chille

6 eggs (size 3), separated

Salt (to taste)

White pepper (to taste)

¼ teaspoon cream of tartar

Generously butter a 1½L; 50 fl oz; 1½-quart soufflé dish with 15g; ½ oz of butter. Make a collar for the dish by cutting a piece of aluminium foil 2.5cm; 1 inch longer than the diameter of the dish. Fold in half lengthwise and generously butter one side of the foil with 15g; ½ oz of butter. Wrap around top edge of dish, butter side in, to come about 5cm; 2 inches above the edge. Secure foil in place with string or heatproof tape. Set aside.

Preheat oven to Gas mark 5; 190°C: 375°F.

Melt 70g; 2½ oz butter in a heavy saucepan over medium heat. When melted, stir in flour, dry mustard, and cayenne pepper. Cook, stirring constantly, for about 1 minute or until butter is well incorporated into the flour. Whisk in warm milk and cook, stirring constantly, for about 2 minutes or until thick. Remove from heat and stir in cheese, sweetcorn, pepper, and chille.

Beat egg yolks and stir into batter until well blended. Add salt and white pepper.

Beat egg whites with cream of tartar until soft peaks form. Stir one quarter of the egg whites into cheese mixture. Gently fold in remaining egg whites. Pour into prepared soufflé dish. Place in preheated oven. Bake 40 minutes for a runny centre, about 1 hour for a firm centre, or until golden brown and well puffed. Carefully remove from oven. Gently remove collar and serve immediately.

Mexican Cheese Enchiladas with Red Chille Salsa

Serves 6.

225g; 8 oz grated Queso Blanco (available in Latin-American markets; if unavailable, use the same amount of mild cheddar cheese)

115g; 4 oz grated cheddar cheese

3 tablespoons minced jalapeño chille

60g; 2 oz chopped, drained, canned green chilles

12 corn tortillas

Red Chille Salsa

Combine 170g; 6 oz Queso Blanco and cheddar cheese with jalapeño and green chilles. Set aside.

Preheat oven to Gas mark 5; 190°C; 375°F.

Wrap tortillas in aluminium foil and place in preheated oven. Bake for about 10 minutes or until warm and pliable.

Salsa into bottom of a 13-inch by 9-inch by 2-inch baking dish. Set aside.

Pour 250mL; 8 fl oz of Red Chille Salsa into bottom of a 33cm; 13-inch by 23cm; 9-inch by 5cm; 2-inch baking dish. Set aside.

When tortillas are warm, remove from oven and unwrap. Dip each tortilla into Red Chille Salsa. Lay flat and place an equal portion of cheese mixture down the centre of each tortilla. Roll tightly and place, seam-side down, into prepared dish. When all tortillas are rolled, pour remaining salsa over the top. Cover tightly with foil and place in preheated oven. Bake for 15 minutes or until cheese has melted and tortillas are very hot.

Preheat grill.

Remove tortillas from oven, unwrap, and sprinkle tops with remaining Queso Blanco. Place under grill and cook for 1 minute or until cheese is melted and bubbly. Serve immediately.

Red Chille Salsa

Makes approximately 470mL; 16 fl oz.

8 dried hot red chilles

230g; 8 oz minced onion

1 clove garlic, peeled and minced

1 tablespoon vegetable oil

1 tablespoon plain flour

500mL; 16 fl oz chicken stock or water

Salt (to taste)

Soak chilles in cold water to cover for 20 minutes or until softened. Drain. Remove stems and seeds.

Place chilles, onion, and garlic in a blender or a food processor fitted with the metal blade. Process until mixture becomes a paste.

Heat oil in a heavy frying pan over medium heat. When hot, add chille paste, lower heat, and sauté for 5 minutes or until slightly cooked. Stir in flour and cook for 1 minute or until incorporated. Add chicken stock or water and salt, and cook for 15 minutes or until slightly thickened and flavours are well incorporated. The salsa may be made in advance and stored, covered and refrigerated, until ready to use.

69

Chille Cheese Strata

Serves 6.

Cheese Strata has been an American kitchen staple for generations; this is my hot version.

340g; ¾ lb cheddar cheese, grated

340g; ¾ lb cheddar cheese, grated

340g; ¾ lb Fontina cheese, grated

45g; 1½ oz minced spring onions

2 tablespoons minced sun-dried tomatoes packed in oil

500mL; 16 fl oz milk

250mL; 8 fl oz double cream

4 eggs (size 3)

1 teaspoon dry mustard

1 teaspoon Worcestershire sauce

¼ teaspoon cayenne pepper

Pinch ground nutmeg

Salt (to taste)

Pepper (to taste)

12 slices homemade-style white bread, quartered

20g; ¾ oz grated Parmesan cheese

Combine cheeses, spring onions, chilles, and sun-dried tomatoes. Set aside.

Combine milk, cream, eggs, dry mustard, Worcestershire sauce, cayenne pepper, nutmeg, salt, and pepper. Set aside.

Generously butter a 2L; 6½ pt soufflé dish. Place a layer of bread on the bottom of prepared soufflé dish. Cover with one third of the cheese mixture. Make 2 more layers of bread and cheese, then end with a final layer of bread. Pour egg mixture over the top and refrigerate for 4 hours.

Preheat oven to Gas mark 4; 180°C; 350°F.

Place Cheese Strata in preheated oven and bake for 30 minutes. Remove from oven and sprinkle with Parmesan cheese. Return to oven and bake for an additional 30 minutes or until a knife inserted in the centre comes out clean and the Strata is puffed and lightly brown. Serve immediately.

Note: Remember when seasoning the Strata that cheese and tomatoes are salty.

70

Chilli

Serves 6 to 8.

Everyone has their own version of chilli. To this basic, meatless version you can add any meat or poultry you desire. For a vegetarian meal, add chopped mixed vegetables. You can serve chilli with or without rice, but always with extra Hot Sauce on the side.

450g; 1 lb dried pinto or pink beans or red kidney beans

3 tablespoons corn oil

170g; 6 oz chopped onion

130g; 4½ oz chopped green pepper

2 tablespoons minced jalapeño chille

2 tablespoons minced garlic

800g; 28 oz chopped, canned tomatoes

20g; ¾ oz chilli powder

2 tablespoons ground cumin

½ teaspoon ground oregano

½ teaspoon cayenne pepper

Salt (to taste)

Pepper (to taste)

Wash and clean beans. Soak in cold water to cover for at least 4 hours, changing water at least 3 times. Drain. Place in cold water to cover by 7.5cm; 3 inches in a heavy saucepan over high heat. Bring to a boil. When boiling, lower heat and simmer for 1 hour or until just tender.

Heat oil in a heavy frying pan over medium-high heat. When hot, add onion, pepper, jalapeño, and garlic. Fry, stirring frequently, for about 4 minutes or until vegetables are soft. Stir into beans. Add remaining ingredients and cook for another 45 minutes or until flavours are well blended and chilli is quite thick. Serve hot.

Note: If using ground or diced meat or poultry, brown it with the onion before adding to the beans.

Maccheroni all'Arrabbiata

Serves 6.

A simple, traditional, hot Italian recipe.

60mL; 2 fl oz extra-virgin olive oil

6 cloves garlic, peeled and sliced

3 whole dried hot red chilles

1kg; 2½ lb canned Italian plum tomatoes with basil

600g; 1¼ lb mostaccioli, ziti, penne, or rigatoni

20g; ¾ oz grated Parmesan cheese

Salt (to taste)

Pepper (to taste)

Chopped parsley (optional)

Heat oil in a large, heavy saucepan over medium-high heat. When hot, add garlic and chilles. Lower heat and fry, stirring frequently, for about 5 minutes or until garlic is golden and chilles are deep brown. Remove garlic and chilles and discard. (If you want a very spicy sauce, let 1 chille pod remain.)

Add tomatoes. Raise heat and bring to a boil. Lower heat and simmer for about 25 minutes or until sauce has thickened.

Cook pasta according to package directions for al dente. When done, drain well. Pour drained pasta into tomato sauce. Add cheese, salt, and pepper and cook for an additional 3 minutes, stirring constantly. Pour onto a warm serving platter and sprinkle with parsley, if desired. Serve immediately with extra cheese, if desired.

Red Chille Couscous

Serves 6.

Throughout the Middle East and Africa, couscous is a nutritious staple. It makes a wonderful vegetarian meal.

2 dried hot red chilles

285g; 10 oz whole-grain or refined couscous

2 tablespoons extra-virgin olive oil

¼ teaspoon ground cinnamon

Salt (to taste)

900g; 2 lb mixed fresh vegetable chunks (such as onion, carrot, cauliflower, broccoli, and courgette)

340g; 12 oz cooked, well-drained beans or chick-peas

Tomato Sauce

Soak dried chilles in boiling water to cover for 20 minutes or until soft. When soft, stem, seed, and cut into a fine julienne. Set aside.

Soften couscous according to package directions. When softened, drain off any excess liquid. Stir in julienned chilles, olive oil, cinnamon, and salt. When well combined, scrape into top half of a large steamer lined with muslin. Arrange vegetables and beans over the top. Cover and steam for 20 minutes or until couscous is cooked and vegetables are tender. Remove to a serving platter and serve with Tomato Sauce.

Tomato Sauce

Makes about 600mL; 1 pt.

450g; 1 lb peeled, cored, seeded, and chopped tomatoes

45g; 1½ oz minced coriander

2 tablespoons minced spring onions

1 tablespoon minced garlic

1 tablespoon minced pickled hot peppers

2 tablespoons olive oil

1 teaspoon fresh lemon juice

½ teaspoon ground cumin

¼ teaspoon dried red pepper flakes

Salt (to taste)

Combine all ingredients in a nonreactive bowl. Cover and allow to marinate at room temperature for at least 2 hours before serving.

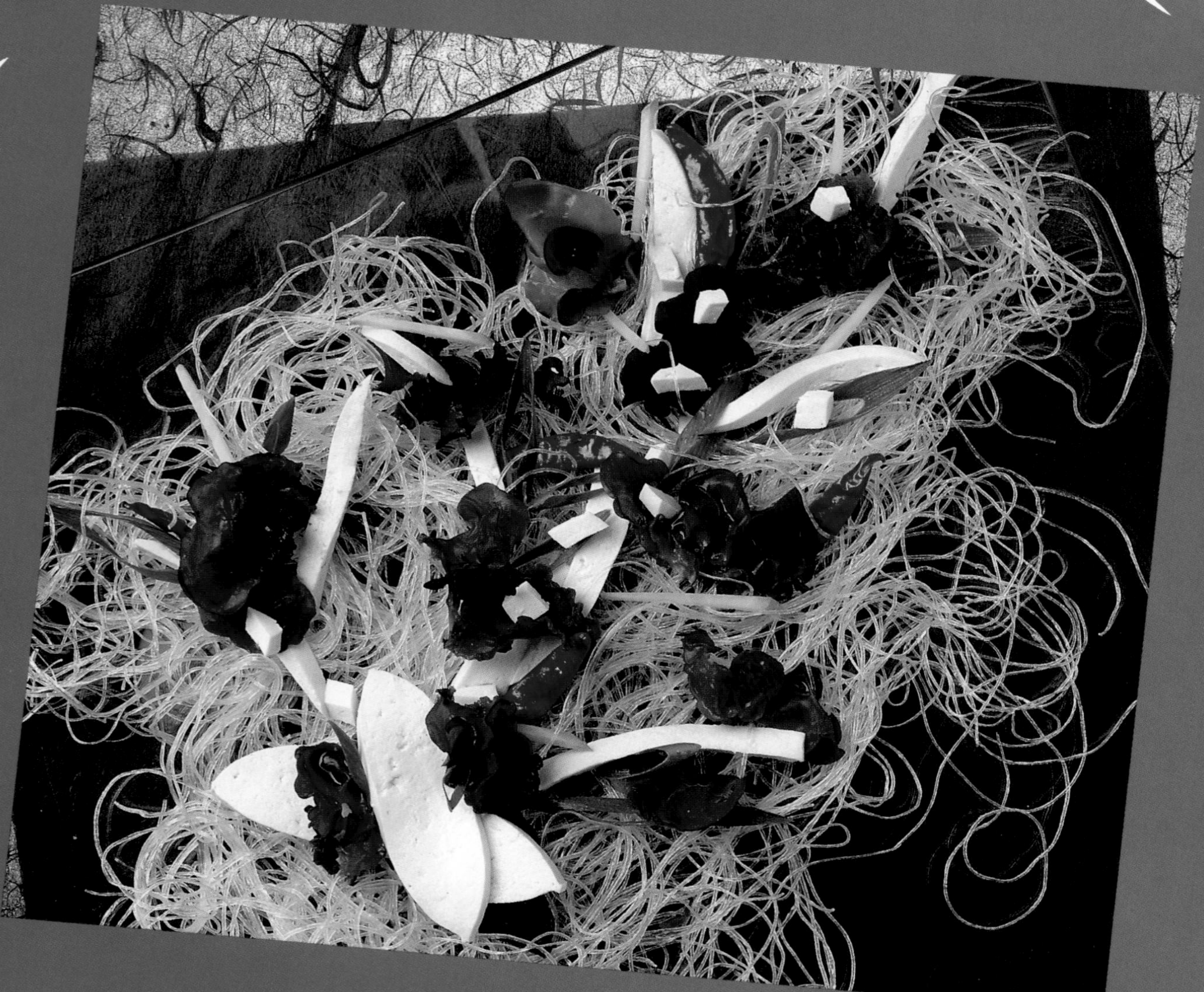

Ants Climbing a Tree

Serves 6.

In Chinese cooking, this is traditionally made with finely minced pork (the ants), however, I use minced tofu as a great vegetarian replacement. You can also use finely minced chicken or turkey, if desired.

10g; ⅓ oz dried tree ear mushrooms (available in Asian markets)

2 dried hot red chilles

355mL; 12 fl oz vegetable or chicken stock

2 tablespoons hot bean sauce (available in Asian markets)

2 tablespoons dry sherry

2 tablespoons soy sauce

230g; ½ lb Chinese cellophane noodles (available in Asian markets)

3 tablespoons peanut oil

230g; ½ lb minced tofu

45g; 1½ oz chopped spring onions

1½ tablespoons minced fresh ginger

Place tree ears in warm water to cover for 30 minutes or until soft. When soft, drain and cut into a fine julienne. Set aside.

Place chilles in boiling water to cover for 20 minutes or until softened. When soft, drain and stem, seed, and cut into a fine julienne. Set aside.

Combine stock, hot bean sauce, sherry, and soy sauce. Set aside.

Soak cellophane noodles in warm water to cover for about 15 minutes or until soft and transparent. Drain well and cut into 7.5 to 10 cm; 3- to 4-inch pieces.

Heat oil in a wok over high heat. When hot, add tofu and stir-fry for about 2 minutes or until tofu browns. Immediately add spring onions, ginger, chilles, and tree ears and toss to combine. Add seasoned stock and stir-fry for 3 minutes. Immediately stir in cellophane noodles. Lower heat to medium and cook uncovered, for about 3 minutes or until almost all the liquid has been absorbed. Taste and adjust seasonings with soy sauce, if necessary. Serve immediately.

Curry

Serves 6.

I am forever indebted to the marvellous Madhur Jaffrey, Indian cook without peer, for sharing her vast knowledge of her native cuisine through her many cookbooks. This is my basic curry sauce, which can be used as a basis for meat, poultry, shellfish, or vegetables.

10 whole cloves

2 teaspoons cumin seeds

2 teaspoons coriander seeds

1 teaspoon black mustard seed (available at Indian markets)

1 tablespoon cardamon seeds

¼ teaspoon fennel seeds

1 5cm; 2-inch cinnamon stick

1 teaspoon turmeric

¼ teaspoon cayenne pepper

70g; 2½ oz clarified butter (see page 72)

255g; 9 oz diced onion

2 tablespoons minced garlic

1 tablespoon minced fresh ginger

1 dried hot red chille

180mL; 6 fl oz Coconut Milk

355mL; 12 fl oz stock (vegetable, meat, poultry, or fish), as required

1 tablespoon fresh lemon juice

340g; 12 oz diced, peeled, cored, and seeded plum tomatoes (optional)

Salt (to taste)

Pepper (to taste)

60g; 2 oz plain yoghurt

120mL; 4 fl oz double cream

1 teaspoon Garam Masala (see page 13)

Place cloves, cumin, coriander, mustard, cardamon, and fennel seeds, cinnamon stick, and turmeric in a heavy frying pan over medium heat. Fry, stirring constantly, for about 3 minutes or until nicely roasted and aromatic. Remove from heat and together with the cayenne pepper grind in a spice grinder (a small coffee grinder used only for spices). Set aside.

Heat clarified butter in a heavy saucepan over medium-high heat. When hot, add the onions and fry, stirring frequently, until onions are a deep red brown, turning heat down about halfway through the browning process so that onions do not burn. Stir in garlic and ginger and fry for an additional 3 minutes or until well incorporated into onions. Add spices, chille, and Coconut Milk, and cook for 2 minutes. Raise heat. Add stock, lemon juice, and tomatoes, if using. Bring to a boil. Lower heat and season with salt and pepper. Simmer for about 20 minutes or until sauce has reduced somewhat and is slightly thickened. Add yoghurt, a tablespoon at a time, stirring constantly to blend well. At this point, add whatever you are going to curry—meat, poultry, shellfish, or vegetables (see note). Cook, stirring frequently, until tender: approximately 45 minutes for lamb, 20 minutes for chicken, and 10 to 15 minutes for shellfish or vegetables.

Stir in cream and Garam Masala and cook for another 5 minutes or until well blended. Serve immediately with basmati or brown rice and any chutney you desire. You can also add chopped coriander and/or chopped, unsalted roasted cashews as garnishes.

Note: Before adding to curry, 700g to 900g; 1½ to 2 lb of boned meat or poultry should be cut into bite-size pieces and lightly browned in clarified butter.

900g; 2 lb of shellfish should be cut into bite-size pieces and flesh removed from shells.

Vegetables should be washed, peeled, and trimmed, when necessary, and cut into bite-size pieces. You will need about 900g to 1.15kg, 8 to 10 cups of prepared vegetables. If using vegetables that require different cooking times, add them one at a time, with those requiring the most cooking added first.

76

Chapter Four

Side Dishes

Barbecued Cajun-Spiced Vegetables

Pepperonata

Vegetable Gumbo

Annie's Fried Potatoes

Southwestern Potato Fritters

Sweetcorn Pie

Szechuan Squash

Sautéed Cabbage and Bow Ties

Grilled Tomatoes with Coriander Pesto

Zap's Onion Rings

Jalapeño Cheese Scones

Homemade Sausage

Grilled Cajun-Spiced Vegetables

Barbecued Cajun-Spiced Vegetables

Serves 6.

2 red peppers

2 yellow peppers

2 green peppers

2 large sweet onions, peeled

1 large courgette

60mL; 2 fl oz olive oil

2 tablespoons fresh lemon juice

Cajun Spice Seasoning

Preheat barbecue or grill.

Stem and seed peppers. Trim off all the white membrane and cut into strips.

Slice onions crosswise into 0.5cm; ¼-inch slices.

Wash and trim courgette. Cut on the bias into 1cm; ½-inch slices.

Combine oil and lemon juice with 2 tablespoons Cajun Spice Seasoning. Pour over vegetables and toss to coat well. Place on preheated barbecue (or under grill). Cook, turning frequently, for about 4 minutes or until slightly soft and nicely brown. Serve immediately.

Note: You may use any vegetables you desire in place of those listed above.

Cajun Spice Seasoning

Makes approximately 6 tablespoons.

2 tablespoons paprika

1 tablespoon cayenne pepper (or to taste)

2 teaspoons salt (or to taste)

2 teaspoons ground black pepper

2 teaspoons unsalted onion powder

1 teaspoon unsalted garlic powder

1 teaspoon dried oregano

1 teaspoon dried thyme

¼ teaspoon crushed, dried bay leaf

¼ teaspoon dried lemon peel

Combine spices and lemon peel. Store, covered, in a cool, dark place for up to 1 month.

Pepperonata

Serves 6.

A great Italian vegetable dish.

2 small aubergines

3 tablespoons coarse (sea) salt

700g; 1½ lb very ripe plum tomatoes

3 medium-size sweet onions

2 red peppers

2 green peppers

3 tablespoons extra-virgin olive oil

3 cloves garlic, peeled and sliced

2 dried hot red chilles

30g; 1 oz minced Italian parsley

Salt (to taste)

Pepper (to taste)

3 tablespoons red wine vinegar

Wash aubergines. Trim and cut into 2.5cm; 1-inch slices. Lay slices in a nonreactive dish and generously sprinkle with coarse salt. Allow to set for 30 minutes. Wash and pat dry. Cut into chunks and set aside.

Place tomatoes in rapidly boiling water for 10 seconds. Remove skins, core, and cut into quarters. Set aside.

Peel and cut onions into 0.3cm; ⅛-inch slices.

Wash, core, and seed peppers. Cut into strips. Set aside.

Heat oil in a heavy saucepan over medium-high heat. When hot, add garlic and chilles. Lower heat and fry for about 5 minutes or until garlic is golden and chilles are nicely browned. Remove garlic and chilles and discard. Raise heat to medium. Add aubergine, onion, and peppers to oil. Cook, stirring constantly, for 5 minutes. Drain tomatoes and stir into pot. Add parsley, salt, and pepper, and cook for 15 minutes or until vegetables are just soft and flavours have been blended.

Stir in vinegar. Raise heat and boil for 3 minutes. Remove from heat and serve hot or cold.

Vegetable Gumbo

Gumbo is a rich, tasty Cajun stew.

Serves 6.

2 tablespoons bacon fat or vegetable oil

170g; 6 oz chopped onion

85g; 3 oz chopped spring onions, including green part

1 tablespoon minced garlic

130g; 4½ oz diced red pepper

130g; 4½ oz diced green pepper

2 tablespoons minced fresh parsley

1 teaspoon minced fresh thyme

1 teaspoon minced fresh marjoram

1 teaspoon freshly ground pepper

½ teaspoon ground mace

½ teaspoon cayenne pepper (or to taste)

1 bay leaf

450g; 1 lb diced fresh okra

340g; 12 oz fresh sweetcorn

230g; 8 oz diced, peeled, cored, and seeded tomatoes

170g; 6 oz fresh baby lima beans or flageolot beans

355mL; 12 fl oz chicken stock

Salt (to taste)

Heat bacon fat or vegetable oil in a heavy frying pan over medium heat. When hot, add onion, spring onions, and garlic. Fry, stirring frequently, for about 5 minutes or until onions are golden. Add peppers, parsley, herbs, and spices and continue to cook for 3 minutes. Add vegetables, stock, and salt. Raise heat and bring to a boil. Lower heat and cook for about 15 minutes or until vegetables are tender and flavours are well blended. Remove and discard bay leaf. Serve immediately.

Annie's Fried Potatoes

Serves 6.

My Irish friend, Anne Mc-Donogh, is a superb Indian cook. This recipe is based on her secret recipe for fried potatoes.

60mL; 2 fl oz peanut oil

2 teaspoons black mustard seeds

2 teaspoons sesame seeds

½ teaspoon fennel seeds

570g; 1¼ lb diced, cooked white potatoes

1 teaspoon black pepper

¼ teaspoon cayenne pepper

Salt (to taste)

Heat oil in a large, nonstick frying pan. When hot, add mustard, and sesame and fennel seeds, stirring constantly. As soon as the seeds begin to burst, add potatoes to the pan. Fry, stirring constantly, for 5 minutes. Stir in black and cayenne peppers and salt. Cover and cook for 7 minutes or until potatoes are quite brown. Turn potatoes. Cover and cook for another 5 minutes or until potatoes are crispy.

Southwestern Potato Fritters

Serves 4 to 6.

450g; 1 lb baking potatoes

1 tablespoon olive oil

2 large Anaheim chilles

170g; 6 oz cooked sweetcorn

85g; 3 oz grated sharp cheddar cheese

230g; 8 oz masa harina

1 teaspoon baking powder

¼ teaspoon Tabasco sauce or Hot Sauce (see page 12) (or to taste)

Salt (to taste)

Approximately 250mL; 8 fl oz cold water

Approximately 60mL; 2 fl oz peanut oil

230g; 8 oz sour cream

45g; 1½ oz chopped fresh coriander

Preheat oven to Gas mark 6; 200°C; 400°F.

Scrub potatoes and pat dry. Rub with olive oil. Prick with a fork and place in preheated oven. Bake for about 45 minutes or until a knife inserted into the centres meets no resistance. Remove from oven. Immediately split open and scrape potato from skins into a mixing bowl. Set aside.

Stick a long-handled fork into the stems of the chilles. Place chilles directly over open flame on top of stove and roast, turning frequently, until completely charred. Place in a thick plastic bag and seal. Allow to steam for 5 minutes. Remove from the bag and gently scrape off skin. Cut open and remove seeds and membrane. Finely chop and add to potatoes.

Stir in sweetcorn, cheese, masa harina, baking powder, Tabasco or Hot Sauce, and salt. Add water, no more than 250mL; 8 fl oz, a bit at a time until mixture is firm and holds together. Form into patties about 6cm; 2½-inches round and 2cm; ¾-inch thick.

Heat peanut oil in a heavy frying pan over medium-high heat. When hot, add fritters. Lower heat to medium and fry fritters for about 4 minutes per side or until golden. Drain on paper towels and serve hot, garnished with sour cream and coriander.

Sweetcorn Pie

Serves 6.

60g; 2 oz butter

3 tablespoons finely diced red pepper

1 tablespoon minced jalapeño chille (or to taste)

500mL; 16 fl oz canned cream-style sweetcorn

60g; 2 oz yellow cornmeal

120mL; 4 fl oz milk

1 tablespoon maple syrup

Salt (to taste)

115g; 4 oz grated cheddar cheese

Preheat oven to Gas mark 6; 200°C; 400°F.

Use 15g; ½ oz of the butter to grease a 1.2L; 2 pt casserole. Heat remaining butter in a heavy saucepan over medium heat. When hot, add pepper and chille. Lower heat and sauté for 3 minutes or until soft.

Whisk together sweetcorn, cornmeal, milk, maple syrup, and salt. When well combined, stir in 70g; 2½ oz cheddar cheese. When well blended, pour into prepared casserole. Sprinkle top with remaining cheddar cheese and place casserole in preheated oven. Bake for 30 minutes or until pie is set, puffed, and golden. Serve immediately.

Szechuan Squash

Serves 6.

3 large courgettes

2 teaspoons salt

2 dried hot red chilles

3 tablespoons rice wine vinegar (available in Asian markets)

1 tablespoon soy sauce

1½ tablespoons caster sugar

1 tablespoon cornflour

4 tablespoons sesame oil (available in Asian markets)

2 tablespoons peanut oil

2 teaspoons Szechuan peppercorns (available in Asian markets)

2 tablespoons minced fresh ginger

2 tablespoons minced spring onion

Cut courgettes crosswise into 0.5cm; ¼-inch slices. Place in a colander and toss with salt. Allow to drain for 30 minutes. Rinse under cold running water and pat dry.

Stem and seed chilles. Cut into a fine julienne.

Combine rice wine vinegar, soy sauce, sugar, and cornflour. Set aside.

Heat oils in a wok over medium-high heat. When hot, stir in peppercorns and chilles. Stir-fry for 1 minute. Add courgettes, ginger, and spring onion and stir-fry for 30 seconds. Add rice wine vinegar mixture and stir for another minute. Taste and adjust seasonings. Serve immediately.

Sautéed Cabbage and Bow Ties

Serves 6.

I was given this recipe by a Czech cook.

115g; 4 oz butter

2 teaspoons cracked black pepper

½ teaspoon caraway seeds

1 teaspoon grated orange rind

570g; 1¼ lb shredded red cabbage

1 tablespoon light soft brown sugar

Pinch cayenne pepper

230g; ½ lb bow tie noodles, cooked

Salt (to taste)

Heat butter in a deep, heavy frying pan over medium-high heat. When hot, add pepper and caraway seeds. Stir to blend. Add orange rind and cook for 1 minute.

Stir in cabbage. Cook, stirring frequently, for about 4 minutes or until cabbage is cooked and beginning to brown. Stir in sugar and cayenne until well combined. Add bow ties and salt. Cook, stirring frequently, for another 3 minutes or until heated through. Taste and adjust seasonings. Serve immediately.

Grilled Tomatoes with Coriander Pesto

Serves 6.

This pesto uses Southwestern flavours instead of the usual basil and parmesan cheese of the Italian original.

6 firm, ripe tomatoes

Coriander Pesto

2 tablespoons fresh bread crumbs

1 teaspoon cracked black pepper

1 tablespoon olive oil

Preheat grill.

Wash tomatoes. Cut in half crosswise. Coat each half with Coriander Pesto. Sprinkle with bread crumbs and pepper. Drizzle with olive oil.

Place on a tray under preheated grill and cook for 3 minutes or until heated through and the tops are bubbly. Serve immediately.

Coriander Pesto

Makes about 355mL; 12 fl oz.

85g; 3 oz fresh coriander leaves

1 teaspoon minced serrano chille

1 clove garlic, peeled and chopped

30g; 1 oz pine kernels

70g; 2½ oz freshly grated dry goat cheese (or grated Parmesan)

1 teaspoon fresh lime juice

60mL; 2 fl oz olive oil

Puree coriander, chille, and garlic in a food processor fitted with the metal blade. With motor running, add pine kernels, then cheese, until well combined. Pour in olive oil in a steady stream until mixture is thick. Scrape from bowl. Stir in lime juice. Cover and refrigerate for up to 24 hours until ready to use.

87

Zap's Onion Rings

Serves 6.

I make these in honour of my son's friend, who prefers hot things to sweet things.

4 to 5 large sweet onions

1L; 32 fl oz buttermilk

425g; 15 oz plain flour

3 tablespoons cornflour

3 tablespoons cornmeal

35g; 1¼ oz chille powder

1 tablespoon hot paprika

1 teaspoon cayenne pepper

1 teaspoon ground cumin

1 teaspoon caster sugar

Salt (to taste)

Approximately 1.5L; 48 fl oz vegetable oil

Peel onions and cut crosswise into 0.3cm; ⅛-inch-thick slices. Pull slices apart into rings. Place in a nonreactive bowl and soak in buttermilk for 1 hour.

Combine flour, cornflour, cornmeal, chille powder, paprika, cayenne pepper, cumin, sugar, and salt. Pour onions into a colander and allow to drain. Dredge rings, a few at a time, in the seasoned flour.

Heat oil in a deep-fry pan to 182°C; 360°F on a food thermometer. Fry onion rings, a few at a time, for about 30 seconds until golden and crisp. Drain on paper towels and serve hot.

88

Jalapeño Cheese Scones

Makes about 2 dozen.

285g; 10 oz plain flour

115g; 4 oz cornmeal

1½ tablespoons baking powder

1 teaspoon bicarbonate of soda

½ teaspoon cracked black pepper

½ teaspoon salt

¼ cup cold vegetable shortening

320mL: 12½ fl oz milk

340g; 12 oz grated cheddar cheese

85g; 3 oz minced jalapeño chille

Preheat oven to Gas mark 7; 220°C; 425°F.

Generously grease a baking sheet.

Combine dry ingredients. Cut in shortening to make a coarse meal. Stir in milk, cheese, and chille, if using, until just combined and dough is sticky.

Drop batter by the spoonful about 2.5cm; 1 inch apart onto the prepared baking sheet. Place in preheated oven and bake for about 15 minutes or until golden. Serve hot.

Homemade Sausage

Makes about 1.15kg; 2½ pounds.

900g; 2 lb very lean, coarsely minced pork

115g; ¼ lb coarsely minced salt pork

2 tablespoons minced fresh parsley

1 tablespoon minced fresh sage

1 teaspoon minced fresh thyme

1 teaspoon minced fresh marjoram

1 teaspoon cayenne pepper (or to taste)

½ teaspoon cracked black pepper

¼ teaspoon ground nutmeg

Pinch ground allspice

120mL; 4 fl oz cold water (optional)

Salt to taste (optional)

Combine all ingredients until well blended. If mixture seems to need moisture, add water 1 tablespoon at a time.

Make a small test patty and fry in a small frying pan over medium heat until well cooked. Taste and adjust seasonings.

Shape remaining sausage into rolls about 15cm; 6 inches long and 5cm; 2 inches in diameter. Tightly wrap in cling film. Refrigerate for about 4 hours until firm enough to cut into 1cm; ½-inch-thick rounds.

Place rounds in a cold, heavy saucepan over medium heat. Cover and fry, turning once, for about 10 minutes or until well cooked and golden brown.

Note: You may make the sausage and cut into 1cm; ½-inch-thick rounds. Place freezer paper between each round. Wrap again tightly and freeze for future use.

**Guacamole, Fruit Chutney, and
East Indian Salsa**

Chapter Five

Condiments, Sauces, and Seasonings

East Indian Onion Relish

Thai Vegetable Relish

Hot and Sweet Applesauce

Fruit Chutney

Pepper Jelly

Mom's Chille Sauce

Salsa Variations: Red, Green, Fruit, and East Indian

Guacamole

Basic Mexican Red Chille Sauce

Basic Mexican Green Chille Sauce

Spiced Vinegar or Oil

Jerk Seasoning

East Indian Onion Relish

Makes approximately 500mL; 16 fl oz.

This condiment is almost always served with every Indian meal. I use it to enliven sandwiches and cold roast meats or poultry.

2 large sweet onions (such as Maui or Vidalia)

2 tablespoons fresh lemon juice

1 tablespoon fresh orange juice

1 tablespoon minced fresh coriander

1 teaspoon salt (or to taste)

½ to 1 teaspoon cayenne pepper

¼ teaspoon paprika

Peel onions. Cut crosswise into paper-thin slices. Separate slices into rings. Place in a nonreactive container with remaining ingredients. Toss to coat. Cover and allow to marinate for at least 1 hour, tossing occasionally. Leftover relish may be stored, tightly covered and refrigerated, for up to 1 week.

Thai Vegetable Relish

Makes about 1L; 32 fl oz.

100g; 3½ oz caster sugar

120mL; 4 fl oz white wine vinegar

120mL; 4 fl oz cold water

½ teaspoon salt (or to taste)

85g; 3 oz tiny cauliflower florets

170g; 6 oz julienned carrots

140g; 5 oz julienned cucumbers

45g; 1½ oz finely chopped spring onion

2 tablespoons chopped fresh coriander

2 serrano chilles, stemmed and sliced crosswise

Bring sugar, vinegar, water, and salt to a boil in a medium-size saucepan over high heat. Boil, stirring frequently, for about 2 minutes or until sugar has dissolved. Remove from heat and allow to cool to room temperature.

Combine vegetables in a nonreactive container with a cover. When vinegar mixture is cool, pour over vegetables. Toss to combine. Cover and marinate at room temperature for 24 hours before serving. The relish may be kept, covered and refrigerated, for up to 1 week.

Hot and Sweet Applesauce

Makes about 700mL; 24 fl oz.

6 whole cloves garlic, unpeeled

6 whole shallots, unpeeled

1 tablespoon vegetable oil

8 tart green apples (such as Granny Smith), peeled, cored, and quartered

120mL; 4 fl oz chicken stock

2 tablespoons champagne vinegar

1 teaspoon balsamic vinegar

1 teaspoon grated orange rind

½ teaspoon ground cumin

¼ teaspoon ground coriander

3 tablespoons maple syrup

Salt (to taste)

Cayenne pepper (to taste)

Preheat oven to Gas mark 4; 180°C; 350°F.

Rub unpeeled garlic and shallots with oil. Place on a baking sheet in preheated oven and bake for 20 minutes or until quite soft and well browned. Remove from oven and set aside to cool.

Place apples, chicken stock, vinegars, orange rind, and spices in a heavy saucepan over medium-high heat. Cook, stirring frequently, for about 15 minutes or until apples are mushy.

Squeeze garlic and shallots out of their skins and into the apple mixture. Add maple syrup. Stir to blend and cook for an additional 5 minutes. Season with salt and cayenne pepper. Serve warm.

Fruit Chutney

Makes approximately 2L; 64 fl oz.

570g; 1¼ lb diced dried fruit, such as apricots, peaches, or pears or a mixture of dried fruits or 900g; 2 lb diced, firm, unripe fresh fruit such as peaches, pears, mangoes, apples, or cranberries or a mixture of fresh fruits

250mL; 8 fl oz cider vinegar

120mL; 4 fl oz fresh orange juice

230g; 8 oz light soft brown sugar (see note)

200g; 7 oz caster sugar (see note)

1 lemon, seeded and chopped

1 orange, seeded and chopped

170g; 6 oz chopped red onion

1 tablespoon minced garlic

170g; 6 oz yellow raisins

30g; 1 oz minced crystallized ginger

2 dried hot red chilles, seeded and chopped

1 tablespoon minced fresh ginger

1 teaspoon ground cinnamon

¼ teaspoon ground coriander

If using dried fruit, allow to soak in boiling water to cover for 1 hour or until well plumped. Drain well.

Combine vinegar, orange juice, sugars, lemon, orange, onion, and garlic in a heavy saucepan over medium-high heat. Bring to a boil. Boil, stirring constantly, until sugars are dissolved. Add remaining ingredients and bring to a boil. When boiling, lower and simmer for 30 minutes or until thick. Pour into a nonreactive container and allow to cool to room temperature. Store, covered and refrigerated, for up to 3 months.

Note: Additional sugar may be added depending upon the tartness of the fruits used.

Pepper **J**elly

Makes 2L; 64 fl oz.

3 large green peppers

3 hot green chilles (your choice)

355mL; 12 fl oz white vinegar

1.25kg; 2¾ lb caster sugar

3 to 4 drops green food colouring (optional)

1 package liquid pectin

Stem, seed, and chop peppers and chilles. Mince in a food processor fitted with the metal blade with 120mL; 4 fl oz vinegar. Combine with remaining vinegar in a nonreactive saucepan over medium-high heat. Bring to a boil. Lower heat and simmer for 10 minutes.

Line a colander with several layers of muslin. Place over a large nonreactive saucepan. Slowly pour pepper mixture into lined colander and allow it to strain into the saucepan. Discard solids.

Bring liquid to a boil over high heat. Add food colouring, if desired. Add liquid pectin and bring to a rolling boil. Boil for 2 minutes. Remove from heat. Remove any residue from top and pour into hot, sterilized jars. Seal with screw-top lids. Store in a cool, dark place for up to 6 months.

Mom's **C**hille **S**auce

Makes about 700mL; 24 fl oz.

My mother canned quarts of this chille sauce at the end of summer. I make just a small batch to keep on hand in the refrigerator.

1 dried hot red chille

5 very ripe large tomatoes, peeled and cored

2 large onions, chopped

1 green pepper, cored, seeded, and chopped

100g; 3½ oz caster sugar

250mL; 8 fl oz cider vinegar

1 teaspoon ground cinnamon

1 teaspoon ground cloves

1 teaspoon dry mustard

½ teaspoon cayenne pepper (or to taste)

2 teaspoons salt (or to taste)

1 tablespoon cornflour (optional)

Soak chille in hot water to cover for about 20 minutes or until soft. Stem and chop.

Place chille, tomatoes, onion, and pepper in a food processor fitted with the metal blade, and process until finely chopped. Place in a heavy saucepan over medium heat with sugar, vinegar, cinnamon, cloves, dry mustard, and cayenne pepper. Cook, stirring constantly, for about 5 minutes or until sugar has dissolved. Bring to a boil, stirring constantly. Lower heat and simmer for 30 minutes. Stir in salt and cook for 5 minutes. If sauce is not thick enough, dissolve cornflour in 1 tablespoon water and stir into sauce. Cook for an additional 5 minutes. Remove from heat and allow to cool.

When cool, place in a non-reactive container. Cover and refrigerate for up to 1 month. Serve as a garnish for meat, poultry, fish, or on sandwiches.

95

Salsa Variations

With the increasing popularity of Tex-Mex, Cali-Mex, and other Mexican influences on America's fast food, everyone has a salsa to use with corn chips, tacos, and enchiladas. Here are a couple of variations on a familiar theme.

Red Salsa

Makes about 600mL; 1 pt.

3 large ripe tomatoes, peeled, seeded, and finely chopped

85g; 3 oz finely chopped red onion

45g; 1½ oz chopped spring onions

45g; 1½ oz chopped fresh coriander

2 teaspoons minced serrano chille

2 cloves garlic, peeled and chopped

1 tablespoon fresh lime juice

1 tablespoon olive oil

Salt (to taste)

Combine all ingredients in a nonreactive bowl and allow to marinate for at least 2 hours before serving. Taste and adjust seasonings with salt and extra lime juice, if necessary.

Green Salsa

Makes approximately 500mL; 16 fl oz.

12 fresh tomatillos (do not use canned tomatillos to make salsa) or 3 large green tomatoes (available in Latin-American markets and gourmet food shops)

60g; 2 oz minced shallots

1 clove garlic, peeled and minced

2 tablespoons minced fresh coriander

1 serrano chille, stemmed, seeded, and chopped

2 teaspoons lime juice

Salt (to taste)

Remove husks from tomatillos. Wash well and wipe dry. (Or core and chop tomatoes.) Place tomatillos in a heavy frying pan over medium heat. Cook, shaking pan, for about 5 minutes or until skin begins to burst. Immediately remove from heat. Cut tomatillos into pieces.
Combine tomatillos with remaining ingredients in a food processor fitted with the metal blade. Process, using quick on-and-off turns, until just chopped. Do not puree. Taste and adjust seasonings. If salsa is bitter, add maple syrup, 1 teaspoon at a time, until appropriate flavour is reached.

Fruit Salsa

Makes approximately 1L; 32 fl oz.

340g; 12 oz finely diced fresh pineapple, papaya, mango, melon, tart apple, or other firm-fleshed fruit

170g; 6 oz finely diced jicama, Jerusalem artichoke, chayote, or cucumber

130g; 4½ oz finely diced red, green, or yellow pepper (see note)

30g; 1 oz minced shallots

1 hot red or green chille, seeded and minced

1 clove garlic, peeled and minced

2 tablespoons minced fresh coriander

1 teaspoon minced fresh mint

3 tablespoons fresh lime juice

1 tablespoon olive oil

Salt (to taste)

Maple syrup (to taste)

Combine all ingredients and allow to marinate for at least 2 hours before serving. Taste and adjust seasonings with salt and maple syrup, adding just a little at a time, if necessary.

Note: Use the colour pepper that will best enhance the colour of the completed salsa.

East Indian "Salsa"

Makes approximately 600mL; 1 pt.

This is almost Tex-Mex in its flavours, but it is a common Indian relish taught to me by an Indian friend.

340g; 12 oz diced ripe tomatoes

255g; 9 oz diced red onion

85g; 3 oz chopped fresh coriander

1 tablespoon fresh lime juice

½ teaspoon cayenne pepper

¼ teaspoon ground cumin

Salt (to taste)

Combine all ingredients in a nonreactive bowl. Allow to marinate for 1 hour before serving.

Guacamole

Makes about 700mL; 24 fl oz.

Avocados are one of my favourite foods. I use them in salads, sandwiches, and sauces, as their mellow flavour is a great balancer to hot foods. To use guacamole to calm a fiery menu, eliminate the hot chilles and use only 1 tablespoon of the onion. It will still be delicious.

4 large ripe avocados

230g; 8 oz cored, peeled, seeded, and diced ripe tomatoes

85g; 3 oz finely diced red onion

1 serrano chille, seeded and minced

1 clove garlic, peeled and minced

2 tablespoons fresh lime juice

1 tablespoon minced fresh coriander

Salt (to taste)

Pepper (to taste)

Peel and chop avocado. Combine with remaining ingredients. Serve immediately.

Basic Mexican Red Chille Sauce

Makes about 1L; 32 fl oz.

40 dried hot red chilles

1 chopped onion

2 tablespoons minced garlic

2 teaspoons minced fresh oregano

1 teaspoon minced fresh epazote (available in Latin-American markets)

Salt (to taste)

Place chilles in cold water to cover for about 10 minutes or until soft. Drain, stem, and seed.

Place in a heavy saucepan with water to cover. Add remaining ingredients and bring to a boil over high heat. Lower heat and simmer for 30 minutes. Pour into a blender in batches and puree until smooth. Store, covered and refrigerated, for up to 1 month.

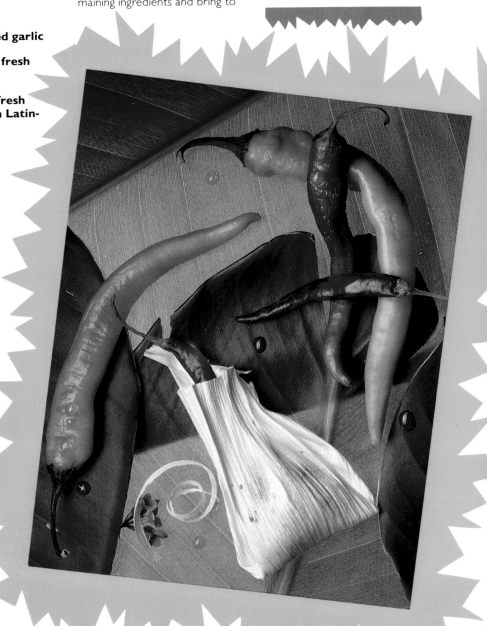

Basic Mexican Green Chille Sauce

Makes about 700mL; 24 fl oz.

450g; 1 lb fresh, mildly hot green chilles, such as anaheim

170g; 6 oz chopped onion

2 tablespoons vegetable oil

1 clove garlic, peeled and chopped

250mL; 8 fl oz chicken stock

Salt (to taste)

Preheat oven to Gas mark 8; 230°C; 450°F.

Place chilles on a baking sheet in preheated oven and bake for 20 minutes or until well charred. Remove from oven and allow to cool until able to handle. Peel, stem, and seed.

Heat oil in a heavy saucepan over medium heat. When hot, add onion and garlic. Sauté, stirring frequently, for about 5 minutes or until quite soft. Add chilles, chicken stock, and salt. Cook for about 20 minutes or until quite thick.

Pour into a blender and process until smooth. Store, covered and refrigerated, for up to 2 weeks.

Spiced Vinegar or Oil

Makes about 1L; 32 fl oz.

1L; 32 fl oz fine wine vinegar or fine olive oil

30g; 1 oz whole peppercorns

2 tablespoons chopped fresh ginger

2 tablespoons allspice berries

1 whole dried chille (your choice)

1 tablespoon salt (or to taste)

1 teaspoon cayenne pepper

Combine all ingredients in a heavy saucepan over medium heat. Bring to a simmer. Immediately turn flame to lowest setting. Keep vinegar or oil just hot for 30 minutes. Pour into a sterilized container. Cover and let stand for 24 hours. Strain. Discard solids. Pour spiced vinegar or oil into a clean container. Cover and refrigerate. The vinegar or oil may be kept, refrigerated, for up to 6 months.

Jerk Seasoning

Makes approximately 500mL; 16 fl oz.

This is the most basic seasoning sauce for the Jamaican-style pit barbecue called jerk. It is used to season meat, poultry, or fish for outdoor barbecuing or oven baking. First, generously rub the food to be jerked with fresh lime juice. Then marinate it in jerk seasoning for at least 4 hours.

115g; 4 oz tamarind pulp (available in Asian, Latin-American, or Caribbean markets)

120mL; 4 fl oz warm water

12 habañero chilles, stemmed

12 serrano chilles, stemmed

60g; 2 oz chopped shallots

85g; 3 oz chopped spring onions

60mL; 2 fl oz peanut oil

1 tablespoon fresh lime juice

1 tablespoon vinegar

1 tablespoon ground allspice

2 teaspoons salt (or to taste)

1 teaspoon ground cinnamon

1 teaspoon cracked black pepper

½ teaspoon ground nutmeg

Place tamarind and warm water in a nonreactive container. Allow to sit for 1 hour. Strain and discard seeds and pulp.

Combine with remaining ingredients in a blender and process until smooth. Store, covered and refrigerated, for up to 1 week.

Chapter Six

Desserts

Molé Waffles with Coffee Ice Cream and Bittersweet Sauce

Caramel Dumplings

Warm Gingerbread with Ginger Cream

Spicy Apple Cake

Pumpkin Custard

Ginger Poached Oranges

Baked Apple Crêpe with Chille Glaze

Molé Waffles with Coffee Ice Cream and Bittersweet Sauce

Makes 6 waffles.

215g; 7½ oz plain flour

1 tablespoon baking powder

1 tablespoon cocoa powder

½ teaspoon ground cinnamon

Pinch ground nutmeg

Tiny pinch cayenne pepper

60g; 2 oz unsweetened chocolate

3 eggs (size 3), separated

60g; 2 oz butter

140g; 5 oz caster sugar

1 teaspoon pure vanilla extract

300mL; 1 pt buttermilk

85g; 3 oz finely chopped, roasted almonds

1 scoop coffee ice cream per person

Bittersweet Sauce

120mL; 4 fl oz double cream, whipped

Preheat waffle iron.

Combine dry ingredients and set aside.

Melt chocolate in the top half a double boiler over hot water. Keep warm.

Beat egg whites until stiff; set aside.

Cream butter and sugar. Add melted chocolate and vanilla. When well combined, beat in egg yolks. Add buttermilk alternately with dry ingredients. Stir in almonds. When well combined, fold in beaten egg whites.

Bake in preheated waffle iron according to manufacturer's directions. Keep waffles warm as you bake all the batter. You will need one half a waffle per person. When all waffles are made, set aside those you will need. Tightly wrap and freeze those that you won't use.

Cut each waffle into quarters. Place a scoop of coffee ice cream on top of 1 quarter and cover it with another, pushing down to slightly squash the ice cream. Drizzle with Bittersweet Sauce and place a dollop of whipped cream on top. Serve immediately.

Bittersweet Sauce

Makes about 500mL; 16 fl oz.

285g; 10 oz bitter chocolate

250mL; 8 fl oz milk

60mL; 2 fl oz double cream

60g; 2 oz light soft brown sugar

45g; 1½ oz butter

Coarsely chop chocolate and place in a heat-resistant bowl. Bring milk, cream, sugar, and butter to a boil in a medium-size saucepan over medium heat. Immediately pour over chocolate and beat to blend. Serve warm or at room temperature. The sauce may be stored, covered and refrigerated, for up to 2 weeks.

Caramel Dumplings

Serves 6 to 8.

215g; 7½ oz plain flour

2 teaspoons baking powder

1 teaspoon ground cinnamon

½ teaspoon ground nutmeg

¼ teaspoon ground cardamon

Pinch ground coriander

60g; 2 oz butter

400g; 14 oz caster sugar

1 teaspoon pure vanilla extract

120mL; 4 fl oz milk

500mL; 16 fl oz boiling water

⅛ teaspoon salt

115g; 4 oz pecans

Combine flour, baking powder, and spices. Set aside.

Cream 30g; 1 oz of the butter and 100g; 3½ oz sugar. When well creamed, stir in vanilla. Add milk alternately with dry ingredients and stir until just blended. Set aside.

Place 100g; 3½ oz of the sugar in a cast-iron frying pan over medium-high heat. Cook, stirring constantly, for about 5 minutes or until sugar is golden brown and caramelized. Care-fully stir in the boiling water. When well blended, stir in the remaining sugar, butter, and salt. When well combined, stir in pecans.

Drop batter by the spoonful into the hot syrup. When all batter has been dropped into the syrup, lower heat and cover. Cook, covered, for about 25 minutes or until dumplings are cooked through and syrup is thick. Serve hot with double cream, if desired.

Warm **G**ingerbread with **G**inger **C**ream

Makes 1 8- by 12-inch cake.

3 **cups all-purpose flour**

2 **teaspoons ground ginger**

1 **teaspoon ground cinnamon**

½ **teaspoon ground cloves**

¼ **teaspoon ground mace**

½ **cup unsalted butter**

1¼ **cups light brown sugar**

¾ **cup molasses**

1 **large egg**

1 **teaspoon pure vanilla extract**

1 **teaspoon grated orange rind**

2 **teaspoons baking soda**

1 **cup buttermilk**

½ **cup yellow raisins (optional)**

¼ **cup minced crystallized ginger (optional)**

Ginger Cream

Preheat oven to 350°F.

Grease and flour an 8- by 12-inch cake pan.

Sift dry ingredients together and set aside.

Using an electric mixer, cream butter and sugar. When well combined, add molasses, egg, vanilla, and orange rind.

Dissolve soda in buttermilk and add to the creamed ingredients alternately with the dry ingredients. Stir in raisins and crystallized ginger if using. Pour into the prepared pan and place in preheated oven. Bake for 35 minutes or until a cake tester inserted into the center comes out clean.

Cut into squares and serve with Ginger Cream.

Ginger Cream

Makes 2 cups.

1½ **cups heavy cream**

½ **cup sour cream**

3 **tablespoons confectioner's sugar**

¼ **teaspoon ground ginger**

2 **tablespoons dark rum**

½ **teaspoon pure vanilla extract**

¼ **cup minced crystallized ginger**

Combine creams, sugar, and ground ginger. Place in the freezer for about 10 minutes.

Beat mixture with an electric mixer until soft peaks form. Add rum and vanilla and beat until stiff. Fold in crystallized ginger and serve immediately.

Spicy Apple Cake

Makes 1 10-inch cake.

2	cups applesauce
1	cup molasses
2	teaspoons baking soda
3	cups all-purpose flour
2	teaspoons ground ginger
1	teaspoon ground cinnamon
½	teaspoon ground cloves
½	teaspoon ground nutmeg
⅛	teaspoon salt
4	large eggs
1⅓	cups sugar
⅔	cup vegetable oil

Preheat oven to 325°F.

Grease and flour a 10-inch tube pan.

Bring applesauce to a boil in a heavy saucepan over medium-high heat. When boiling, stir in molasses and baking soda. Immediately remove from heat and set aside to cool.

Sift together flour, spices, and salt. Set aside.

Beat eggs until light yellow. Gradually beat in sugar. Beat for 5 minutes or until quite thick. Gradually add oil. Alternately stir in applesauce and dry ingredients. When well combined, pour into the prepared pan and place in preheated oven. Bake for 1 hour and 15 minutes or until a cake tester inserted into the center comes out clean. Cool in pan on a wire rack for 15 minutes. Then remove the cake from the pan and continue cooling on wire rack.

Pumpkin Custard

Serves 6.

1	tablespoon unsalted butter
3	tablespoons chopped pecans
2	tablespoons chopped crystallized ginger
3	teaspoons light brown sugar
1½	cups heavy cream
1	cup milk
1	3-inch vanilla bean
3	large eggs
2	large egg yolks
½	cup superfine sugar
½	teaspoon ground ginger
¼	teaspoon ground cinnamon
	Dash ground cloves
⅔	cup pumpkin purée
	Mint leaves, for garnish (optional)

Melt butter in a small saucepan over low heat. When melted, stir in pecans and crystallized ginger. Sauté for 4 minutes or until pecans being to glaze. Remove mixture from heat and place an equal portion in the bottom of 6 individual soufflé dishes or ramekins. Sprinkle each with ½ teaspoon brown sugar. Place molds in a shallow baking dish and set aside.

Preheat oven to 325°F.

Place heavy cream and milk in a heavy sauté pan over medium heat. Scrape the insides from the vanilla bean into the cream-milk mixture. Bring just to the boiling point and remove from heat.

Beat eggs and egg yolks until well blended. Add sugar and continue beating until pale yellow and thick. Stir in spices. Pour in cream-milk mixture in a constant, steady stream, beating continuously. When well blended, beat in pumpkin puree. When smooth, pour equal portions into prepared molds. Pour enough boiling water into baking dish to come halfway up the sides of the molds.

Place in preheated oven and bake for about 40 minutes or until custard is set and golden. Remove from oven and let stand for about 30 minutes before serving, either warm or chilled in their baking dishes, or unmolded, garnished with a mint leaf, if desired.

To unmold, place each soufflé dish in boiling water for about 20 seconds. Place serving plate on top and quickly invert custard onto it.

Ginger Poached Oranges

Serves 6.

8 seedless navel oranges

15g; ½ oz butter

65g; 2¼ oz caster sugar

1 285g; 10-oz jar of preserved Canton ginger (available in Asian markets)

120mL; 4 fl oz dry white wine

250mL; 8 fl oz fresh orange juice

1 tablespoon fresh lemon juice

1 tablespoon fresh lime juice

2 tablespoons chopped fresh mint

Remove orange rind, orange part only, from 3 oranges. Cut into a very fine julienne.

Melt butter in a small frying pan over medium heat. When melted, add 1½ tablespoons sugar and julienned orange rind. Sauté, stirring constantly, for about 4 minutes or until orange rind is nicely glazed. Remove from pan and cool on grease proof paper. Set aside.

Place ginger with its liquid in a food processor fitted with the metal blade. Using quick on-and-off turns, process until finely chopped.

Combine ginger with the wine, citrus juices, and remaining sugar in a medium-size saucepan over high heat. Bring to a simmer. Remove from heat and allow to cool for about 5 minutes.

Peel all the oranges, making certain that they are free of membrane. Cut crosswise into 0.3cm; ⅛-inch slices. Place in a shallow nonreactive bowl. Pour citrus syrup over oranges. Cover and refrigerate for 8 hours, basting occasionally. Serve cold, garnished with glazed orange rind and mint.

Baked Apple Crêpe with Chille Glaze

Serves 6 to 8.

45g; 1½ oz butter

135g; 4¾ oz caster sugar

½ teaspoon ground cinnamon

2 tablespoons Calvados

1 tablespoon apple juice

4 tart apples, peeled, cored, and sliced

4 eggs (size 3), separated

120mL; 4 fl oz double cream

70g; 2½ oz plain flour

¼ teaspoon salt

250mL; 8 fl oz milk

30g; 1 oz melted butter, cooled

Chille Glaze

Preheat oven to Gas mark 5; 190°C; 375°F.

Use 15g; ½ oz butter to generously grease a 35.5cm; 14-inch tart tin (or 2 20cm; 8-inch cake tins). Sprinkle with 2 tablespoons sugar and set aside.

Melt remaining butter in a nonstick frying pan over medium heat. When melted, add 1 tablespoon sugar, cinnamon, Calvados, and cider. Stir to combine. Cook for about 3 minutes or until sugar has dissolved. Add apples and sauté

for about 5 minutes or until just tender and slightly glazed. Remove from heat and set aside.

Combine egg yolks with cream. When well combined, stir in remaining sugar, flour, and salt. Gradually stir in milk and melted butter. Beat egg whites until stiff and fold into the batter. Pour batter into prepared pan(s). Push apple slices down into the top and drizzle with any pan juices. Place in preheated oven and bake for 25 minutes or until puffed and golden. Cut into serving pieces and drizzle with Chille Glaze.

Chille Glaze

Makes approximately 180mL; 6 fl oz.

15g; ½ oz butter

1 teaspoon minced fresh ginger

1 teaspoon minced serrano chille

20g; ¾ oz caster sugar

500mL; 16 fl oz apple juice

2 tablespoons Calvados

Melt butter in a heavy saucepan over medium-high heat. When melted, add ginger and chille and sauté for 2 minutes. Stir in sugar and continue to cook for 4 minutes or until sugar has begun to brown. Carefully add cider and Calvados and bring to a boil. Boil for about 15 minutes or until reduced to 180mL; 6 fl oz. Remove from heat and strain through a fine sieve. Keep warm until ready to use.

Chapter Seven

Drinks

Mexican Coffee

Spiced Tea

Virgin Mary

Mint Punch

Glögg

Ginger Beer

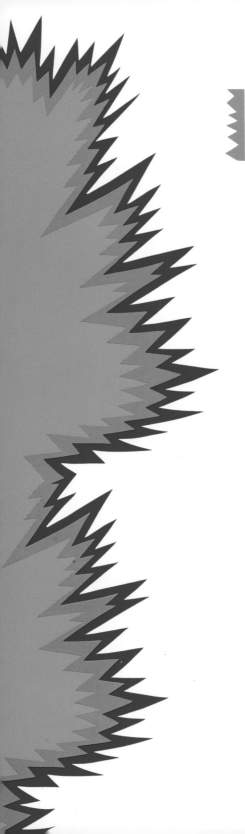

Mexican Coffee

Makes 1.5L; 48 fl oz.

1.5L; 48 fl oz water

170g; 6 oz dark brown soft sugar

1 small orange studded with 8 cloves

2 5cm; 2-inch cinnamon sticks

3 tablespoons ground coffee

Combine water and brown sugar in a heavy saucepan over medium heat. Cook, stirring constantly, for about 3 minutes or until sugar has dissolved. Add orange, cinnamon sticks, and coffee and bring to a boil. Lower heat and simmer for 3 minutes. Remove from heat. Cover and allow to sit 1 minute. Strain and serve immediately with cream on the side, if desired.

Variation:

Proceed as above, replacing coffee with ground espresso. Melt 1 ounce bitter chocolate in 250mL; 8 fl oz double cream in another small saucepan over medium heat. When well combined, pour into a blender and whip until slightly thick and frothy. Scoop onto the top of each serving of coffee and garnish with ground cinnamon or cocoa powder.

Spiced Tea

Serves 6.

3 tablespoons tea leaves

6 whole cloves

1 cardamon seed

1 5cm; 2-inch cinnamon stick

Pinch ground nutmeg

1 teaspoon minced crystallized ginger

½ teaspoon grated orange rind

½ teaspoon grated lemon rind

1.5L; 48 fl oz boiling water

Combine tea, spices, ginger, and citrus rinds. Allow to set for 1 hour.

Place in a warm teapot and pour freshly boiled water over all. Cover and steep for 3 to 5 minutes. Serve with sugar and a slice of orange or lemon as a garnish, if desired.

Virgin Mary

Makes 1L; 32 fl oz.

1L; 32 fl oz tomato juice

2 tablespoons fresh lemon juice

1 teaspoon Worcestershire sauce

1 teaspoon Hot Sauce, (or to taste) (see page 12)

Dash celery salt

Salt (to taste)

Cracked black pepper (to taste)

6 celery sticks for garnish

Combine all ingredients except celery sticks. Pour into ice-filled highball glasses and garnish with a celery stick. Serve immediately.

Note: You can add alcohol to this base to make a Bloody Mary: 60mL; 2 ounces vodka or pepper vodka per serving. Or a Danish Mary: 60mL; 2 ounces aquavit per serving.

Mint Punch

Serves 6.

200g; 7 oz caster sugar

250mL; 8 fl oz cold water

2 teaspoons chopped fresh ginger

6 cloves

1 7.5cm; 3-inch cinnamon stick

85g; 3 oz chopped fresh mint leaves

250mL; 8 fl oz fresh orange juice

60mL; 2 fl oz fresh lemon juice

1 tablespoon fresh lime juice

500mL; 16 fl oz cold spearmint tea

700mL; 24 fl oz soda water

6 sprigs fresh mint

Place sugar and water in a medium-size saucepan over high heat. Bring to a boil. Stirring frequently, boil for 5 minutes. Remove from heat. Add ginger, cloves, cinnamon stick, and mint leaves and allow to cool. When cool, strain through a fine sieve into a large jug. Stir in fruit juices and tea. Cover and refrigerate for at least 1 hour. Add 3 cups soda water. Pour into tall glasses over ice and garnish with a sprig of fresh mint.

Glögg

Makes approximately 2L; 64 fl oz.

One Christmas Eve, I made gallons of Glögg for our annual celebration with friends. I didn't really think about its potency, and Christmas Day was difficult for all of us. Serve in moderation.

1L; 32 fl oz red burgundy wine

500mL; 16 fl oz port

120mL; 8 fl oz aquavit

230g; 8 oz light soft brown sugar

8 whole cloves

8 allspice berries

2 cardamon pods

1 10cm; 4-inch cinnamon stick

1 lemon, thinly sliced

1 orange, thinly sliced

Combine all of the ingredients in a heavy, nonreactive saucepan over medium-high heat. Bring to a simmer. Lower heat and cook for 10 minutes. Allow to set for 30 minutes. Strain and reheat. Serve hot, garnished with cinnamon sticks and orange slices, if desired.

Ginger Beer

Makes about 2L; 64 fl oz.

Ginger beer is a favourite Christmas drink throughout the West Indies. This recipe was given to me by Kenneth Roberts, a fine Trinidadian chef.

2 teaspoons dried yeast

60mL; 2 fl oz lukewarm water

120mL; 4 fl oz fresh lime juice

3 tablespoons minced fresh ginger

2 teaspoons grated lime rind

400g; 14 oz caster sugar

2L; 64 fl oz boiling water

Combine yeast and warm water. Stir to dissolve. Let stand 5 minutes or until foamy.
Combine remaining ingredients in a nonreactive container with lid. Stir in yeast until well combined. Cover and store in a warm, draught-free place for 1 week. Strain through a fine sieve. Pour into a clean container. Cover and refrigerate until ready to use. Served chilled over ice, if desired.

Chapter Eight

The Balancers
A Few Cool Foods to Complement Hot Meals

Perfect Rice: Simple, Rich, Pilaf, and Coconut

Coconut Milk and Cream

Roti (Paratha)

Cucumber Yoghurt with Mint and Coriander

Citrus Vinaigrette

Lassi

A Note About Beer

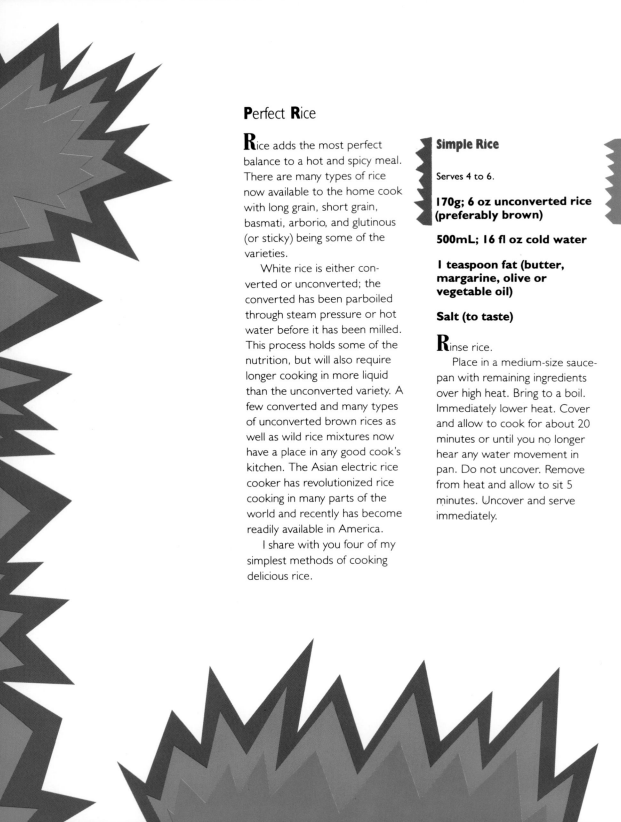

Perfect Rice

Rice adds the most perfect balance to a hot and spicy meal. There are many types of rice now available to the home cook with long grain, short grain, basmati, arborio, and glutinous (or sticky) being some of the varieties.

White rice is either converted or unconverted; the converted has been parboiled through steam pressure or hot water before it has been milled. This process holds some of the nutrition, but will also require longer cooking in more liquid than the unconverted variety. A few converted and many types of unconverted brown rices as well as wild rice mixtures now have a place in any good cook's kitchen. The Asian electric rice cooker has revolutionized rice cooking in many parts of the world and recently has become readily available in America.

I share with you four of my simplest methods of cooking delicious rice.

Simple Rice

Serves 4 to 6.

170g; 6 oz unconverted rice (preferably brown)

500mL; 16 fl oz cold water

1 teaspoon fat (butter, margarine, olive or vegetable oil)

Salt (to taste)

Rinse rice.

Place in a medium-size saucepan with remaining ingredients over high heat. Bring to a boil. Immediately lower heat. Cover and allow to cook for about 20 minutes or until you no longer hear any water movement in pan. Do not uncover. Remove from heat and allow to sit 5 minutes. Uncover and serve immediately.

Rich Rice

Serves 4 to 6.

255g; 9 oz unconverted white or brown rice

30g; 1 oz butter

60g; 2 oz minced shallots or onion

600mL; 2 pt hot stock (chicken, beef, fish, or vegetable)

Salt (to taste)

White pepper (to taste)

Rinse rice and drain well. Set aside.

Melt butter in a heavy saucepan over medium heat. When melted, add shallots and sauté for 3 minutes. Stir in rice and sauté for 3 additional minutes or until rice is glistening and has absorbed some of the butter. Add stock, salt, and pepper and bring to a boil. When boiling, lower heat. Cover and simmer for about 35 minutes or until rice is cooked and liquid is absorbed. Serve immediately.

Note: With this recipe you may add 215g; 7½ oz cooked fresh peas or the same amount of cooked chick-peas, beans, or lentils. You can also add ¼ teaspoon turmeric for a soft, yellow colour.

Rice Pilaf

Serves 6.

10g; ⅓ oz dried porcini mushrooms (or another dried type)

Approximately 1-1.2L; 32-40 fl oz hot stock (chicken, beef, or vegetable)

100g; 3½ oz wild rice

2 tablespoons olive oil

30g; 1 oz minced shallots

2 tablespoons minced celery

1 teaspoon minced fresh herbs (thyme, marjoram, parsley, or a combination of any herbs you like)

170g; 6 oz unconverted rice (preferably brown)

115g; 4 oz nuts (pine, pecans, etcetera) (optional) and/or 85g; 3 oz chopped dried fruit or raisins (optional) or 130g; 4½ oz diced peppers (optional)

Soak mushrooms in boiling water to cover for 45 minutes. Remove mushrooms and chop. Set aside.

Strain liquid through a fine sieve lined with muslin. Measure and place in a heavy saucepan over medium heat. Add stock to make a total of 700mL; 24 fl oz of liquid. Add wild rice and bring to a boil. Lower heat and cook, uncovered, for about 20 minutes or until rice has begun to open. Remove from heat. Drain and reserve rice and liquid separately. Measure liquid and set aside.

Preheat oven to Gas mark 5; 190°C; 375°F.

Heat oil in a heavy casserole over medium heat. When hot, add shallots, celery, and herbs. Sauté for 3 minutes or until soft. Stir in rice and reserved mushrooms. Add reserved wild rice. Measure reserved liquid and add stock to make a total of 700mL; 24 fl oz. Pour into rice. Stir in salt and pepper and any optional ingredient you choose. Cover and place in preheated oven. Bake for 30 minutes or until rice is cooked and liquid is absorbed. Serve immediately or at room temperature.

Note: When serving Rice Pilaf at room temperature, you can add diced al dente vegetables (such as peppers, carrots, celery, and courgettes), nuts, raisins, or any other ingredient you desire to make a colourful side dish.

Coconut Rice

Serves 6.

340g; 12 oz white rice

355mL; 12 fl oz water

250mL; 8 fl oz Coconut Cream (see page 114)

¼ teaspoon turmeric

Salt (to taste)

Rinse rice and drain well.

Combine with remaining ingredients in a heavy saucepan over medium-high heat. Bring to a boil. When boiling, lower heat. Cover and cook for about 25 minutes or until rice is cooked and liquid is absorbed. Serve immediately.

Note: This recipe may be made with Asian sticky rice and served with fresh fruit as a dessert.

Coconut Milk and Cream

Makes approximately 470mL; 16 fl oz.

Fresh coconut milk and cream often serve to mellow the heat in a recipe. It is easy to make a batch and keep on hand. Please note that the liquid in a coconut is not coconut milk.

1 coconut

Preheat oven to Gas mark 8; 230°C; 450°F.

Prick the eyes of the coconut and drain out the liquid. Place on a baking sheet in preheated oven and bake for 20 minutes. Remove from oven and bang with a hammer. The coconut should break open easily. Peel off brown skin. Remove meat from shell and cut into pieces. Place in a food processor fitted with the metal blade and process until finely minced. Measure minced coconut. Place in a blender with an equal amount of boiling water and process until smooth. Allow to cool slightly.

Line a fine sieve with a double layer of muslin. Place over a bowl. Pour pureed coconut into lined sieve and allow to drain into the bowl. When most of the liquid has drained off, pull up muslin and twist the top part together, pressing hard to squeeze out all the coconut milk. One coconut will usually yield about 500mL; 16 fl oz of coconut milk.

To make coconut cream, follow the same procedure but use half as much boiling water as coconut meat. Store, covered, in the refrigerator for 2 to 3 days.

Roti (Paratha)

Serves 6.

To most Trinidadians, Roti is simply bread. However, it usually refers to a type of bread that is similar to an East Indian *paratha*. This recipe makes an excellent multi-cuisine bread to use with sauces, curries, and dips, or simply to relax the taste buds.

340g; 12 oz plain flour

½ teaspoon baking powder

¼ teaspoon bicarbonate of soda

½ teaspoon salt

Approximately 355mL; 12 fl oz milk

Approximately 115g; 4 oz clarified butter

Sift dry ingredients together. Stir in milk a bit at a time until a stiff dough forms. Place dough on a lightly floured surface and knead for 5 minutes. Form into 6 equal balls.

Again, lightly flour surface. Roll out each ball into a thin 20cm; 8-inch circle. Brush each side with clarified butter. Fold in half, then into quarters. Gently push back into a ball shape. Cover and let stand for 30 minutes.

Heat a large, ungreased cast-iron frying pan until it is very hot. (Test by dripping a drop of water into the centre. If it pops back up, the pan is hot enough.)

On a lightly floured surface, again roll out the balls into thin 20cm; 8-inch circles. Bake the Roti, one at a time, in the hot frying pan for about 3 minutes, turning and brushing with clarified butter frequently until Roti is firm and covered with light brown spots. Remove from heat and enclose with a kitchen towel. With Roti in towel, quickly work Roti with hands, moving back and forth between the hands until pliable. Keep warm wrapped in a towel as you bake remaining Roti. Serve warm.

Cucumber Yoghurt with Mint and Coriander

Serves 6.

Individually, the ingredients in this refreshing relish are palate-cooling tastes. Combined they are a sensational balance to spicy foods of any nation.

4 pickling cucumbers

1 teaspoon salt

450g; 16 oz plain yoghurt

2 tablespoons chopped fresh mint leaves

2 tablespoons chopped fresh coriander

½ teaspoon grated orange rind

Wash and trim cucumbers. Coarsely chop. Place in a colander and sprinkle with 1 teaspoon salt. Allow to drain for 20 minutes. Rinse under cold running water and pat dry.

Toss with remaining ingredients. When well combined, taste and adjust seasonings. Cover and refrigerate until ready to serve.

Citrus Vinaigrette

Makes about 355mL; 12 fl oz.

Lightly steamed al dente vegetables or mixed fresh greens tossed with a light vinaigrette are crisply refreshing with hot meals. You should allow 140g; 5 oz of vegetables per person and about 115g; 4 oz greens.

120mL; 4 fl oz fresh orange juice

2 tablespoons fresh lemon juice

2 teaspoons fresh lime juice

2 teaspoons balsamic vinegar

2 tablespoons minced shallots

1 tablespoon minced fresh parsley

1 tablespoon minced fresh chives

1 teaspoon minced fresh mint

180mL; 6 fl oz peanut oil

Salt (to taste)

White pepper (to taste)

Whisk juices and vinegar together. Stir in shallots and herbs. When well blended, whisk in oil until well combined. Taste and adjust seasonings.

Lassi

Serves 6.

This is a traditional Indian thirst quencher.

450g; 16 oz lemon or plain yoghurt

250mL; 8 fl oz cold water

2 teaspoons fresh lemon or lime juice

3 tablespoons caster sugar

6 ice cubes

6 sprigs fresh mint

Combine yoghurt, water, citrus juice, sugar, and ice cubes in a blender. Process until whipped. Pour into cold glasses and garnish with a fresh mint sprig. Serve immediately.

A Note About Beer

Most hot cuisines have a national beer to accompany their fiery foods. Beer seems to quiet the heat and fan the appetite. Some of the better-known beers are Singha and Amarit from Thailand; Tsing Tao from China; Kingfisher from India; Corona, Superior, and Dos Equis from Mexico. You can, of course, offer any fine-quality beer when serving hot foods.

Some Sample Menus

A Hot and **S**picy **C**ocktail **P**arty

Savannah **C**heese **W**afers

Vegetable **S**amosas with **C**oriander **D**ipping **S**auce

Ginger **S**almon **T**artar

Coconut **P**rawns with **C**alypso **P**unch

Jalapeño **C**orn **M**uffins (split, brushed with mustard, and
filled with sliced smoked ham or turkey)

Laab

Sparkling **W**ines

Beer or **F**ruit **P**unch

A Zesty Buffet

Gado Gado

Hacked Chicken

Barbecued Cajun-Spiced Vegetables

Rice Pilaf (at room temperature)

Tossed Green Salad

Ginger-Poached Oranges with shortbread or any simple
butter cookie

A Wide-Awakening Brunch

Virgin Marys

Jalapeño Cheddar Rajas

Spicy Corn Cheddar Soufflé or
Chille Cheese Strata

Homemade Sausage

Annie's Fried Potatoes

Grilled Tomatoes with Coriander Pesto (or plain, drizzled
with olive oil, salt, and pepper)

Any homemade biscuit, cornbread, or slightly sweetened
breakfast roll or muffin

Mexican Chocolate Coffee

Tea

Lunch

Ginger Consommé

Barbecued Salmon with Lemon Chille Butter

Boiled New Potatoes

Tossed Salad

Baked Apple Crèpe with Chille Glaze

A Supper Menu

Coconut Chicken with Orange Rice

Yellow Beetroot, Mangetout, and Jicama Salad

Spicy Apple Cake with Whipped Cream

Mint Punch

A **F**ormal **D**inner with **S**pice

Chille **S**eviche with **T**ostones

Breast of **D**uck with **L**ime **S**auce and **L**ime **C**hutney

Coconut **R**ice

Any **S**teamed **G**reen **V**egetable

Yellow **B**eetroot, **M**angetout, and **J**icama **S**alad or **T**ossed **M**ixed **G**reens

Pumpkin **C**ustard

Dinner

Red **S**napper à la **V**era **C**ruz

Perfect **R**ice

Guacamole

Lightly **S**teamed **S**quash or **C**hayote with **B**utter, **S**alt, and **P**epper

Sliced **F**resh **F**ruit **D**rizzled with **H**oney and **F**resh **L**ime **J**uice

Mail-Order Sources

Herbs & Spices by Post
PO Box 949
Maldon
Essex
CM9 7PU

Culpeper Ltd.
Hadstock Road
Linton
Cambridge
CB1 6NJ
Tel 0223 894054

*Culpeper supplies herbs and spices and
have shops throughout the UK.*

Kitchen Metrics

For cooking and baking conveniences, use the following for adapting to metric measurement. The table gives approximate, rather than exact, conversions.

Spoons

¼ teaspoon	=	1 milliliter
½ teaspoon	=	2 milliliters
1 teaspoon	=	5 milliliters
1 tablespoon	=	15 milliliters
2 tablespoons	=	25 milliliters
3 tablespoons	=	50 milliliters

Cups

¼ cup	=	50 milliliters
⅓ cup	=	75 milliliters
½ cup	=	125 milliliters
⅔ cup	=	150 milliliters
¾ cup	=	175 milliliters
1 cup	=	250 milliliters

Oven Temperatures

110C (225F/Gas ¼)
120C (250F/Gas ½)
140C (275F/Gas 1)
150C (300F/Gas 2)
160C (325F/Gas 3)
180C (350F/Gas 4)
190C (375F/Gas 5)
200C (400F/Gas 6)
220C (425F/Gas 7)
230C (450F/Gas 8)
240C (475F/Gas 9)
260C (500F/Gas 10)

There are many cookbooks devoted to specific cuisines referred to throughout *Hot!* I would particularly recommend any of those written by Elizabeth Lambert Ortiz, Madhur Jaffrey, Julie Sahni, Paula Wolfert, and my friend, Dean Fearing. For further reading about chilies I would recommend Jean Andrews' definitive *The Domesticated Capsicum* (University of Texas Press).

We gratefully acknowledge the assistance of the following manufacturers and merchants in providing the props and accessories used in this book.

ABC- ABC Carpet & Home
888 Broadway
New York, NY 10003

B   - Bennington Potters, Inc.
PO Box 199
Bennington, VT 05201

FF - Fitz and Floyd, Inc.
2055-C Luna Road
Carrollton, TX 75006

PB - Pottery Barn
700 Broadway
New York, NY 10003

R   - Reminiscence
74 Fifth Avenue
New York, NY 10011

UO - Urban Outfitters
628 Broadway
New York, NY 10012

Z   - Zona
97 Greene Street
New York, NY 10012

17: coasters-Z; 20: plate-FF, fish-R; 23: plate-FF; 24: glass plate-PB, beads-UO; 33: bowls-Z, napkin-PB; 37: plate-FF; 49: plate-FF, figurine-R; 50: plate-FF; 51: large plate-PB, small plates-Z; 52: coasters-PB; 53: plate-FF; 55: banana dish-FF, napkin-UO; 56: plate-FF; 58: spoons-PB, bronze bowl-Z; 60: charger, plate, and napkin-PB; 63: plates-FF; 64: plate and figurine-FF; 67: plate-FF; 68: plates-B; 70: soufflé and plate-B, dishtowel-UO; 77: plate and napkin ring-FF; 81: plate-FF; 82: small black cups-FF; 85: plates-FF; 88: plates-FF; 87: sun disk-UO; 90: bowls-Z; 102: plate and figurine-R; 103: plate-FF; 104: napkin and ring-PB; 100: dish and pumpkin-FF; 107: napkin-PB; 112: dishes-FF

124